Exam Ref AI-900
Microsoft Azure AI
Fundamentals

Julian Sharp

Exam Ref AI-900 Microsoft Azure AI Fundamentals

Published with the authorization of Microsoft Corporation by:
Pearson Education, Inc.

ISBN-13: 978-0-13-735803-8
ISBN-10: 0-13-735803-2

Library of Congress Control Number: 2021947615

1 2021

TRADEMARKS

WARNING AND DISCLAIMER

SPECIAL SALES

For information about buying this title in bulk quantities, or for special sales opportunities (which may include electronic versions; custom cover designs; and content particular to your business, training goals, marketing focus, or branding interests), please contact our corporate sales department at corpsales@pearsoned.com or (800) 382-3419.

For government sales inquiries, please contact governmentsales@pearsoned.com.

For questions about sales outside the U.S., please contact intlcs@pearson.com.

EDITOR-IN-CHIEF
Brett Bartow

EXECUTIVE EDITOR
Loretta Yates

SPONSORING EDITOR
Charvi Arora

DEVELOPMENT EDITOR
Songlin Qiu

MANAGING EDITOR
Sandra Schroeder

SENIOR PROJECT EDITOR
Tracey Croom

COPY EDITOR
Sarah Kearns

INDEXER
Timothy Wright

PROOFREADER
Donna Mulder

TECHNICAL EDITOR
Francesco Esposito

EDITORIAL ASSISTANT
Cindy Teeters

COVER DESIGNER
Twist Creative, Seattle

COMPOSITOR
codeMantra

GRAPHICS
codeMantra

Pearson's Commitment to Diversity, Equity, and Inclusion

Pearson is dedicated to creating bias-free content that reflects the diversity of all learners. We embrace the many dimensions of diversity, including but not limited to race, ethnicity, gender, socioeconomic status, ability, age, sexual orientation, and religious or political beliefs.

Education is a powerful force for equity and change in our world. It has the potential to deliver opportunities that improve lives and enable economic mobility. As we work with authors to create content for every product and service, we acknowledge our responsibility to demonstrate inclusivity and incorporate diverse scholarship so that everyone can achieve their potential through learning. As the world's leading learning company, we have a duty to help drive change and live up to our purpose to help more people create a better life for themselves and to create a better world.

Our ambition is to purposefully contribute to a world where:

- Everyone has an equitable and lifelong opportunity to succeed through learning.

- Our educational products and services are inclusive and represent the rich diversity of learners.

- Our educational content accurately reflects the histories and experiences of the learners we serve.

- Our educational content prompts deeper discussions with learners and motivates them to expand their own learning (and worldview).

While we work hard to present unbiased content, we want to hear from you about any concerns or needs with this Pearson product so that we can investigate and address them.

- Please contact us with concerns about any potential bias at https://www.pearson.com/report-bias.html.

I would like to dedicate this book to my wife, Clare Sharp, for her constant support and demonstrating that learning never stops.

—JULIAN SHARP

Contents at a glance

Contents

Chapter 4   Describe features of Natural Language Processing (NLP) workloads on Azure   115

Acknowledgments

I'd like to thank the following people without whom this book would not have been possible.

Thank you to Loretta and Charvi for your patience and encouragement with this project. To the various editors for your correcting my errors. To Francesco for the quality of the review and your helpful suggestions. To Andrew Bettany for originally recommending me for this book and also for involving me in your Cloud Ready Graduate program, where I learned how to refine the content and the messaging around AI Fundamentals for a wider audience, making this a much better book as a result.

About the author

JULIAN SHARP is a solutions architect, trainer, and Microsoft Business Applications MVP with over 30 years of experience in IT. He completed his MA in Mathematics at the University of Cambridge. Julian has spoken at Microsoft Ignite and many other community events. For the past 15 years, he has been a Microsoft Certified Trainer delivering certification training around Dynamics 365, Azure, and the Power Platform. He has taught thousands of students with a high pass rate. Julian has a passion for Artificial Intelligence to enhance user experience and customer data in the solutions that he designs.

Introduction

Artificial Intelligence (AI) impacts almost everything we do today with devices and computers. The purpose of the AI-900 exam is to test your understanding of the fundamental concepts of AI and the AI services Microsoft provides in Azure. The exam includes high-level concepts for AI and machine learning (ML), as well as the capabilities of particular Azure AI services.

Having a high-level appreciation of AI is important to everyone involved in building and using solutions that make use of AI. There are no prerequisite skills or experience required.

Like the exam, this book takes a high-level approach and is geared toward giving you a broad understanding of the use cases for AI, as well as the common AI services in Azure. Both the exam and the book are at such a high level that there is no coding involved.

This book covers every major topic area found on the exam, but it does not cover every exam question. Only the Microsoft exam team has access to the exam questions, and Microsoft regularly adds new questions to the exam, making it impossible to cover specific questions. You should consider this book to be a supplement to your relevant real-world experience and other study materials. If you encounter a topic in this book that you do not feel completely comfortable with, use the "Need more review?" links you'll find in the text to find more information and take the time to research and study the topic. Great information is available on Microsoft Docs, and in blogs and forums.

Organization of this book

This book is organized by the "Skills measured" list published for the exam. The "Skills measured" list is available for each exam on the Microsoft Learn website: *http://aka.ms/examslist*. Each chapter in this book corresponds to a major topic area in the list, and the technical tasks in each topic area determine a chapter's organization. If an exam covers six major topic areas, for example, the book will contain six chapters.

Preparing for the exam

Microsoft certification exams are a great way to build your resume and let the world know about your level of expertise. Certification exams validate your on-the-job experience and product knowledge. Although there is no substitute for on-the-job experience, preparation through study and hands-on practice can help you prepare for the exam. This book is *not* designed to teach you new skills.

We recommend that you augment your exam preparation plan by using a combination of available study materials and courses. For example, you might use the Exam Ref and another study guide for your "at home" preparation and take a Microsoft Official Curriculum course for the classroom experience. Choose the combination that you think works best for you. Learn more about available classroom training and find free online courses and live events at *http://microsoft.com/learn*. Microsoft Official Practice Tests are available for many exams at *http://aka.ms/practicetests*.

Note that this Exam Ref is based on publicly available information about the exam and the author's experience. To safeguard the integrity of the exam, authors do not have access to the live exam.

Microsoft certifications

Microsoft certifications distinguish you by proving your command of a broad set of skills and experience with current Microsoft products and technologies. The exams and corresponding certifications are developed to validate your mastery of critical competencies as you design and develop, or implement and support, solutions with Microsoft products and technologies both on-premises and in the cloud. Certification brings a variety of benefits to the individual and to employers and organizations.

> **NEED MORE REVIEW?** **ALL MICROSOFT CERTIFICATIONS**
>
> For information about Microsoft certifications, including a full list of available certifications, go to *http://www.microsoft.com/learn*.

Check back often to see what is new!

Quick access to online references

Throughout this book are addresses to webpages that the author has recommended you visit for more information. Some of these links can be very long and painstaking to type, so we've shortened them for you to make them easier to visit. We've also compiled them into a single list that readers of the print edition can refer to while they read.

Download the list at *MicrosoftPressStore.com/ExamRefAI900/downloads*.

The URLs are organized by chapter and heading. Every time you come across a URL in the book, find the hyperlink in the list to go directly to the webpage.

Errata, updates, & book support

We've made every effort to ensure the accuracy of this book and its companion content. You can access updates to this book—in the form of a list of submitted errata and their related corrections—at:

MicrosoftPressStore.com/ExamRefAI900/errata

If you discover an error that is not already listed, please submit it to us at the same page.

For additional book support and information, please visit

MicrosoftPressStore.com/Support

Please note that product support for Microsoft software and hardware is not offered through the previous addresses. For help with Microsoft software or hardware, go to *http://support.microsoft.com.*

Stay in touch

Let's keep the conversation going! We're on Twitter: *http://twitter.com/MicrosoftPress.*

CHAPTER 1

Describe Artificial Intelligence workloads and considerations

Artificial Intelligence (AI) is computers thinking and acting in a way that simulates a human. AI is a technology that takes information from its environment and responds based on what it learns. The goal of AI is to create a machine that can mimic human behavior.

AI is more than learning—it is knowledge representation, reasoning, and abstract thinking. Machine learning (ML) is the subset of AI that takes the approach of teaching computers to learn for themselves, rather than teaching computers all that they need to know. ML is the foundation for modern AI. ML focuses on identifying and making sense of the patterns and structures in data.

ML is about machines' reasoning and decision-making using software that learns from past experiences. ML allows computers to consistently perform repetitive and well-defined tasks that are difficult for humans to accomplish. Over the past few years, machine learning algorithms have proved that computers can learn tasks that are tremendously complicated for machines, demonstrating that ML can be employed in a wide range of scenarios and industries.

AI is now being embedded into the software you use today, sometimes without us realizing it. For example, Microsoft PowerPoint has a feature called Design Ideas that offers suggestions for themes and layouts for slides, and Microsoft Word offers suggestions to rewrite sentences to improve clarity.

This chapter is an overview of how Artificial Intelligence and machine learning can be used in different scenarios and industries ethically.

Skills covered in this chapter:

- Skill 1.1: Identify features of common AI workloads
- Skill 1.2: Identify guiding principles for Responsible AI

Skill 1.1: Identify features of common AI workloads

Artificial Intelligence is software that mimics human behaviors and capabilities. Today, software can use AI to automatically detect and predict actions that machines, and humans, should take.

Microsoft Azure provides a set of services for Artificial Intelligence and machine learning that you can utilize to create your own intelligent solutions. Microsoft Azure AI Fundamentals is a certification that requires you to have entry-level knowledge of AI and ML concepts and knowledge of the related Microsoft Azure services.

> **This skill covers how to:**
> - Describe Azure services for AI and ML
> - Understand Azure Machine Learning
> - Understand Azure Cognitive Services
> - Describe the Azure Bot Service
> - Identify common AI workloads

Describe Azure services for AI and ML

There is a wide and rapidly growing series of services in Azure for AI and ML. There are three services that are the focus of the AI-900 Fundamentals exam:

- **Cognitive Services**   A set of prebuilt services that you can easily use in your applications.
- **Azure Bot Service**   A service to help create and deploy chatbots and intelligence agents.
- **Azure Machine Learning**   A broad range of tools and services that allow you to create your own custom AI.

We will be exploring some of the features and capabilities of these three services in this book. However, these services do not work in isolation; they utilize many other Azure services to deliver solutions such as the following:

- Storage
- Compute
- Web Apps
- HD Insights
- Data Factory
- Cosmos DB
- Azure Functions
- Azure Kubernetes Service (AKS)

Example ML architecture

To explain how Azure services support Azure Machine Learning, consider the scenario of a company that wants to provide recommendations to its users. By providing personalized targeted recommendations, users will more likely purchase more of their products and user satisfaction will increase.

Figure 1-1 shows an example of an ML architecture to support recommendations.

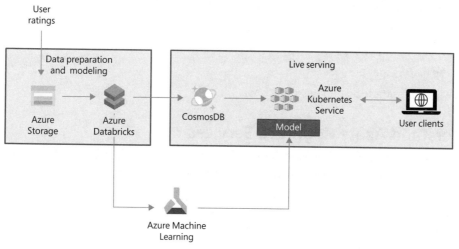

FIGURE 1-1 Example ML architecture

Understand Azure Machine Learning

Azure Machine Learning is the foundation for Azure AI. In Azure Machine Learning, you can build and train AI models to make predictions and inferences.

Training a machine learning model requires lots of data and lots of computing resources. Azure provides many services for preparing data and then analyzing the data.

Azure ML is a platform for training, deploying, and managing machine learning models. We will cover machine learning in more detail in Chapter 2.

Machine learning model types

Machine learning makes use of algorithms to identify patterns in data and take action. The types of machine learning models created from the outputs of the algorithms are as follows:

- **Anomaly Detection**   Finds unusual occurrences.
- **Classification**   Classifies images or predicts between several categories.
- **Clustering (including K-Means Clustering)**   Discovers structures.
- **Regression**   Predicts values.

NOTE **MODEL TYPES**

Understanding the differences between these model types is foundational knowledge for this exam.

For each model type, you will need to understand the following:

- How they work
- What they do
- What they can be used for
- The metrics they produce

We will address these points later in the book.

Understand Azure Cognitive Services

Cognitive Services is a suite of prebuilt AI services that developers can use to build AI solutions. Cognitive Services meets common AI requirements and allow you to add AI to your apps more quickly with less expertise.

Cognitive Services are machine learning models trained by Microsoft with massive volumes of data. While you can build your own custom AI models to perform the same analyses, Cognitive Services allow you to meet many AI requirements easily around processing images and analyzing text. However, Cognitive Services only address a subset of AI requirements. You can create your own machine learning models to meet more complex and specific needs.

Cognitive Services are available as a set of REST APIs for the following capabilities:

- Computer vision, including images and video
- Decision, including Anomaly Detector
- Language, including text analysis and Language Understanding
- Speech, including translation
- Intelligent search, including knowledge mining

Cognitive Services have a broad and growing range of features and capabilities. The Azure AI Fundamentals exam focuses on two of these capabilities:

- Image processing
- Natural Language Processing (NLP)

A great example of the use of Cognitive Services is the free Seeing AI app that uses these two capabilities. Designed for visually impaired people, this app turns the physical environment into an audible experience, locating faces, identifying objects, and reading documents.

Figure 1-2 shows the Seeing AI app in the App Store with sample screenshots and an overview of its features.

We will be looking at the computer vision and Natural Language Processing services of Azure Cognitive Services in Chapters 3 and 4.

FIGURE 1-2 The Seeing AI app

Describe the Azure Bot Service

The *Azure Bot Service* is a cloud-based platform for developing, deploying, and managing bots. Azure Bot Services provide the capabilities known as conversational AI.

Conversational AI is where the computer simulates a conversation with a user or customer. Conversational AI has extended beyond simple chatbots to intelligence agents and virtual assistants like Cortana.

There are two conversational AI services included in the Azure AI Fundamentals exam:

- **QnA Maker**   A tool to build a bot using existing support and other documentation.
- **Azure Bot Service**   Tools to build, test, deploy, and manage bots.

Both QnA Maker and the Azure Bot Service leverage the Language Understanding (LUIS) service in Cognitive Services.

We will look at bots in more detail in Chapter 5.

Identify common AI workloads

There are many use cases for AI. Here we will look at some common AI workloads, describing their features and providing some examples for their use.

Prediction

Prediction, or forecasting, is where the computer identifies patterns in your historical data, and through machine learning associates the patterns with outcomes. You can then use the prediction model to predict the outcome for new data.

Types of predictions include the following:

- **Binary prediction** There are two possible outcomes for a question—yes/no or true/false.
- **Multiple outcome prediction** The question can be answered from a list of two or more outcomes.
- **Numerical prediction** The question is answered with a continuous number, not explicitly limited to a specific range of values.

Prediction models can be used in many varied scenarios. For example, prediction models are found in financial services when evaluating credit applications or evaluating risk. You can use a prediction model to forecast customer churn rate, or to forecast the number of support calls that will be received, or if an opportunity will be converted to a sale.

Following are some questions that could be answered using prediction:

- Will this customer be approved for a $10,000 credit limit?
- Will this flight be delayed?
- Will this flight be on-time, slightly delayed, or very late?
- How many minutes will this flight be delayed by?

Anomaly detection

Anomaly detection analyzes data over time and identifies unusual changes, often for real-time data streams.

Anomaly detection, also known as outlier detection, can find dips and spikes that may indicate a potential issue. Such issues are hard to spot when analyzing aggregate data, as the data points are hidden in the vast volume of data.

Anomaly detection can identify trend changes. Typically, the anomaly will indicate problems such as a sticking valve, payment fraud, a change in the level vibration on a bearing, or errors in text.

Anomaly detection enables pre-emptive action to be taken before a problem becomes critical or adversely affects business operations.

There are several algorithms that can be used for anomaly detection. The Azure Anomaly Detector service selects the best algorithm based on the data, making Anomaly Detector easy to use with a single API call. Anomaly Detector can also run in a Docker container, so it can be deployed at the edge on devices themselves.

Following are some examples of the use of anomaly detection:

- **Monitoring IoT devices**   Checking the telemetry from devices in real-time to find anomalies.
- **Fault detection in electricity systems**   Identifying spikes and dips in the electrical supply.
- **Computer network traffic access attacks**   Detecting unusual network activity both inside the network and on the network perimeter.
- **Financial system fraud**   Identifying potential fraudulent payments from the patterns of payments.
- **Hospital infection**   Recognizing high mortality rates from a particular infection than from other causes of death.
- **Crowd surveillance**   Identifying changing crowd behaviors in complex situations.

Computer vision

Computer vision is the processing of still images and video streams. Computer vision can interpret the image and provide detail and understanding about the image in computer-readable form.

Computer vision can determine if the image contains a specific object (object detection) and can extract details from the image, such as colors or text.

Computer vision can:

- Describe an image
- Categorize an image
- Tag an image
- Detect objects
- Detect faces
- Identify brands and products
- Identify famous people
- Identify landmarks
- Extract text

There are many potential uses for computer vision:

- **Reading text and barcodes**   Reading and identifying text and barcodes every day is not an easy job for a human.

- **Product assembly**   Manufacturers can ensure that assembly of products and components are strictly adhering to standards. For example, pharmaceutical manufacturers can inspect bottles in 360 degrees to ensure correct packaging. They can examine critical features of packaged bottles like cap seal, position, and labels.

- **Monitoring the length of the queue in retail stores**   Retailers can determine if more checkout staff are required.

- **Detecting abnormalities in health scans**   Computer vision can sift the scans, freeing up scarce highly skilled diagnostic staff to analyze the more complex scanned images.

Natural Language Processing

Natural Language Processing (NLP) is the analysis of text to extract information in a form that can be used by a computer.

Natural Language Processing interprets spoken and written text. NLP can analyze the text to determine the language used, determine the sentiment expressed, extract key phrases, and identify key entities and actions.

NLP can be used in many scenarios, such as the following:

- **Decision support**   Assisting users in making decisions from unstructured and rapidly changing data.

- **Bots and intelligent agents**   Understanding the user's question without having been trained in the exact words or phrasing so that a response can be formulated.

- **Translate commands into actions**   Understanding the intent in the user's request and performing the requested action.

- **SPAM detection**   Classifying emails based on the text in the subject and body.

- **Monitoring news**   Extracting relevant news from different feeds that are relevant to the user.

- **Grammar checkers**   Flagging words or phrases and attempting to offer improvements.

Knowledge mining

Knowledge mining is the process of extracting key insights from structured and unstructured data sources.

Knowledge mining uses a combination of AI services, including Azure Cognitive Search, to extract meaning and relationships from large amounts of information. This information can be held in structured and unstructured data sources, documents, and databases. Knowledge mining uncovers hidden insights in your data.

Microsoft provides a Knowledge Mining Solution Accelerator to help you ingest different data and document source, enrich, and index the data, and provides a user interface to explore the results.

Conversational AI

Conversational AI is the process of building AI agents to take part in conversations with humans. Conversational AI is commonly experienced by humans as chatbots on websites and other systems.

AI agents (bots) engage in conversations (dialogs) with human users. Bots use natural language processing to make sense of human input, identify the actions the human wants to perform, and identify the entity on which the actions are to be performed. Bots can prompt the human for the information required to complete a transaction.

There are three common types of bot that you may encounter:

- Webchat
- Telephone voice menus (IVR)
- Personal Digital Assistants

You can use bots in many scenarios, including the following:

- **Customer support**   Handling common questions and inquiries and providing a method for escalating to a human agent.
- **FAQs**   Providing an interactive question and answer service to users over the web or in an app.
- **Online ordering**   Supporting customer ordering and answering common questions about the products or delivery.
- **Travel reservation and booking**   Assisting the customer in finding flights and accommodations that match their requirements and making the booking on their behalf.
- **Healthcare triage**   Guiding the user when triaging a patient to check for symptoms.

Skill 1.2: Identify guiding principles for Responsible AI

Responsible AI is the provision of AI-based solutions to difficult problems without any unintended negative consequences.

This section covers the six principles of Responsible AI. By following these principles, you can ensure that your AI-enhanced solutions will put people first.

EXAM TIP

Make sure you can describe each principle of Responsible AI in a single sentence.

This skill covers how to:

■ Describe the Fairness principle

■ Describe the Reliability & Safety principle

■ Describe the Privacy & Security principle

■ Describe the Inclusiveness principle

■ Describe the Transparency principle

■ Describe the Accountability principle

■ Understand Responsible AI for Bots

■ Understand Microsoft's AI for Good program

NOTE **PRINCIPLES FOR RESPONSIBLE AI**

These principles should be taken into account when creating solutions that use AI. Not every principle will apply to every requirement, but you should check your solution against each principle to see if it applies.

Describe the Fairness principle

The Fairness principle of Responsible AI is concerned with treating all people fairly and reducing unfairness.

A Responsible AI-based solution must operate without giving any unfair advantage to, withholding opportunities from, or allocating resources to a specific group of people. There should be no bias regarding a person's gender, or any other characteristic.

AI systems can reinforce existing stereotypes and underrepresentation. If correctly addressed, AI systems can reduce unfairness.

An AI model should be interpreted to quantify the extent of how data influences the model's prediction to help eliminate bias.

The Fairness principle means:

■ Eliminating bias for gender, age, or ethnicity

■ Removing unfair advantages

■ Preventing unfair allocation of resources

■ Preventing the withholding of information

■ Mitigating bias at each stage of developing and deploying AI systems

Following are some examples where the Fairness principle can have a significant impact:

■ Bank loans/credit decisions

■ Hiring staff

■ Criminal justice system

Describe the Reliability & Safety principle

Reliability & Safety requires the rigorous testing of an AI-based system's functionality and deployment to ensure that it works as expected and eliminates potential risk to human life.

Features of Reliability & Safety are:

- Rigorous testing
- Works as expected
- Eliminates threat of harm to human life

Areas where Reliability & Safety must be applied are as follows:

- Autonomous vehicles
- Healthcare diagnosis

Describe the Privacy & Security principle

Privacy & Security requires that an AI-based system should be secure and respect privacy. AI-based systems typically operate on high volumes of data, including personal data that should not be disclosed.

The reliance on data used in training the model, and new data used for predictions, is subject to privacy rules.

AI systems that run on a user's device should not leak the user's data. One way to achieve this is to run the AI processing on the device and not transfer the personal data to a cloud service.

To be responsible, you should:

- Respect privacy.
- Be secure.
- Avoid disclosing personal data.

Concerns covered by Privacy & Security are as follows:

- **Data origin**   Where has the data come from—is it user or public data?
- **Data use**   Validating that the data you are using has not been corrupted or interfered with.

Describe the Inclusiveness principle

Inclusiveness requires AI-based solutions to empower everyone and supply benefits to all parts of society, regardless of gender, physical ability, ethnicity, sexual orientation, or any other factors.

Inclusiveness means:

- Empowering everyone
- Engaging all communities in the world
- Intentionally designing for the inclusivity principle

Describe the Transparency principle

Transparency is the principle that AI-based solutions should be understandable. Users should be aware of the purpose of an AI-based system, how it operates, its scope, and its limitations.

Transparency is essentially about gaining the trust of users.

Transparency means:

- Defining the purpose of the use of AI in your solution
- Defining the scope of AI in your solution
- Stating the limitations of AI in your solution

AI-based solutions should be understandable. You must be open about how and why you are using AI to users and other stakeholders.

Transparency also means that people can understand the behavior of an AI system; the outputs of an AI algorithm should be able to be interpreted. For example, in some industries, you must be able to explain to regulators how the AI algorithm has generated its results.

Describe the Accountability principle

Accountability requires the people involved in designing and developing AI-based solutions to operate within a clear governance framework due to the impact AI can have on the world.

Accountability requires the people involved in designing and developing AI-based solutions to follow clearly defined ethical policies and legal standards.

Accountability requires that you have:

- Governance framework
- Ethical policies
- Legal standards

Civil liberties are an area where accountability is a crucial factor when determining if and how to use AI—for example, the use of facial recognition.

> **NEED MORE REVIEW? RESPONSIBLE AI**
>
> For more information on Responsible AI, see https://www.microsoft.com/ai/responsible-ai.

Understand Responsible AI for Bots

To illustrate what Responsible AI means, let's look at building a chatbot.

When building a chatbot, you need to consider many of the principles outlined previously. The Transparency principle means that:

- A customer should know they are interacting with a bot.
- The purpose of the bot should be clear.
- The limitations of the bot should be stated.

You can meet this requirement by having a clear welcome message, stating that a bot is responding. It should be possible to seamlessly transfer to a human agent.

Bots operate best when they have a clear purpose. Bots that attempt to handle every possible scenario often perform poorly. The scope of a bot should be reduced to a clearly defined purpose.

> **NEED MORE REVIEW?**   **RESPONSIBLE CONVERSATIONAL AI**
>
> Watch this demo of Responsible Conversational AI at https://aidemos.microsoft.com/responsible-conversational-ai/building-a-trustworthy-bot.

Understand Microsoft's AI for Good program

AI for Good is a Microsoft program that puts AI technology, cloud software, and other resources into the hands of those working to create a more sustainable and accessible world.

AI for Good is enabling advances in healthcare, environmental protection, humanitarian action, cultural heritage, and other areas to make a better world for everyone.

> **NEED MORE REVIEW?**   **AI FOR GOOD**
>
> For more information on AI for Good, see https://www.microsoft.com/ai/ai-for-good.

Chapter summary

In this chapter, you learned some of the general concepts related to Artificial Intelligence. You learned about the features of common AI workloads, and you learned about the principles of Responsible AI. Here are the key concepts from this chapter:

- Artificial Intelligence is a technology that mimics the human brain and uses machines to complete complex tasks that humans find difficult to do.
- Machine learning uses algorithms to discover patterns and structures in existing data, building a model that can be used to take actions (like classify and predict) on unseen data.
- Cognitive Services is a set of prebuilt AI models, trained by Microsoft, that you can use without being a data scientist to add intelligence into your applications.
- Azure Machine Learning is a set of tools and services that you can use to create custom AI models using your own data.
- Azure Bot Service allows you to build and deploy chatbots and intelligence agents.
- Regression is the type of machine learning that predicts values from historical data.
- Classification is the type of machine learning that classifies images or predicts between several distinct categories.

- Clustering discovers structures in data, identifying groups based on similarities in the data.

- Anomaly detection finds unusual occurrences or events in time-series data. Anomaly detection can identify outliers in the data.

- Prediction is the model that predicts outcomes for new data. Predictions are based on historical data. You can have predictions based on regression, classification, and clustering algorithm. Prediction is also known as forecasting.

- Computer vision is the analysis of images and video to extract information that can be used by computers. Computer vision can interpret the contents of the image to classify the image, detect objects in the image, and analyze and describe the image.

- Natural Language Processing is the analysis of speech and text to extract the meaning and intent of words in a way that can be used by computers. Natural Language Processing can interpret text. Natural Language Processing can analyze the text to determine the language used, determine the sentiment expressed, extract key phrases, and identify key entities and actions.

- Conversational AI is used to create applications where AI agents engage humans in conversations (dialogs). Conversational AI is commonly experienced by humans as chatbots on websites.

- Knowledge mining uses a combination of AI services to extract meaning and relationships from large amounts of information. This information can be held in structured and unstructured data sources, documents, and databases. Knowledge mining uncovers hidden insights in your data.

- Responsible AI is the use of AI in solutions without having unintended negative impacts.

- Fairness is the principle that AI-based systems should treat all people fairly and reduce bias.

- Reliability & Safety is the principle that requires rigorous testing of AI-based systems to eliminate harm to human life.

- Privacy & Security is the principle that AI-based systems should be secure and respect privacy of personal data.

- Inclusiveness is the principle that AI-based solutions should empower everyone and supply benefits to all parts of society, regardless of any characteristics or factors.

- Transparency is the principle that AI-based solutions should be understandable, or interpretable. Transparency requires that AI-based systems have a defined purpose and scope and are clear on the limitations of the AI in the solution.

- Accountability is the principle that everyone at every stage in the development of AI-based systems is accountable for the impact that system may have.

Thought experiment

In this thought experiment, demonstrate your skills and knowledge of the topics covered in this chapter. You can find the answers in the section that follows.

You work for Contoso Medical Group (CMG), and your management is interested in using AI in your applications and operations. CMG manages and monitors drug trials, evaluating the efficacy of the treatments.

The CMG IT department is resource-constrained, and they do not have data scientists or skilled AI developers available.

Having timely and accurate responses from patients improves the accuracy of the analysis performed. CMG has created an app to capture and track a patient's daily symptoms. CMG has recently added the capability of the app to take pictures to capture skin conditions. CMG is unable to analyze the images due to the volume of images being captured. CMG is concerned about the amount of data storage for these images, as well as controlling access to the images.

CMG receives a lot of patient history and prescription records that are keyed into CMG's computer systems. These paper records are important information used to track a patient's response to drugs and treatments.

The support department is unable to handle the many inquiries CMG receives. Customers are receiving inconsistent responses depending on whom they speak to and how they are accessing customer support, whether by phone, web, or mobile app.

Your manager has come to you asking for solutions that address these issues. Whatever solution you offer must consider that the medical data in this application is covered under HIPAA, and your manager wants CMG to retain all control of the data. Your manager also wants to carefully control costs.

You have decided that CMG can use AI, but there are several issues that you need to resolve before proceeding.

Answer the following questions:

1. Which AI workload should you use for the customer support department?
2. Which principle of Responsible AI should you employ to gain the trust of users in your bot?
3. Which AI workload should you use to analyze the images for skin conditions?
4. How can you address the storage requirements for the images?
5. Which principle of Responsible AI protects a patient's personal information?
6. Which AI workload could identify adverse reactions to a drug treatment?
7. Which principle of Responsible AI requires rigorous testing of your AI-based app?

Thought experiment answers

This section contains the solutions to the thought experiment. Each answer explains why the answer choice is correct.

1. Conversational AI will allow simple inquiries to be handled by an automated bot. You can create a chatbot for your website, create an assistant for customer service agents, and even enable a bot in a mobile app.

2. Transparency is the principle that AI-based solutions should be understandable. Users should be aware of the purpose of the AI-based system, how it operates, and its scope and limitations. A chatbot should clearly tell the user that it is a bot and what it can and cannot do.

3. Computer vision allows you to analyze images. You can train computer vision with existing images to classify images to determine the type of skin complaint.

4. You can run AI in the app on the mobile device. The image will not need to be stored and will not leave the device. You will instead store the results of the classification along with other symptom data and discard the image.

5. Privacy & Security is concerned with keeping AI-based solutions secure and preventing personal data from being disclosed.

6. Anomaly detection can detect adverse reactions. It can detect where there is a change in trends and can detect unusual readings.

7. Reliability & Safety requires the rigorous testing of an AI-based system's functionality and deployment to ensure that it works as expected and to eliminate potential risk to human life.

CHAPTER 2

Describe fundamental principles of machine learning on Azure

Machine learning (ML) is the current focus of AI in computer science. Machine learning focuses on identifying and making sense of the patterns and structures in data and using those patterns in software for reasoning and decision making. ML uses past experiences to make future predictions.

ML allows computers to consistently perform repetitive and well-defined tasks that are difficult to accomplish for humans. Over the past few years, machine learning algorithms have proved that computers can learn tasks that are tremendously complicated for machines and have demonstrated that ML can be employed in a wide range of scenarios and industries.

This chapter explains machine learning algorithms such as clustering, classification, and regression. The chapter then explains how machine learning works in terms of organizing datasets and applying algorithms to train a machine learning model. The chapter then looks at the process of building a machine learning model and the tools available in Azure.

Skills covered in this chapter:

- Skill 2.1: Identify common machine learning types
- Skill 2.2: Describe core machine learning concepts
- Skill 2.3: Identify core tasks in creating a machine learning solution
- Skill 2.4: Describe capabilities of no-code machine learning with Azure Machine Learning

Skill 2.1: Identify common machine learning types

Machine learning requires lots of data to build and train models to make predictions and inferences based on the relationships in data. We can use machine learning to predict a new value based on historical values and trends, to categorize a new piece of data based on data the model has already seen, and to find similarities by discovering the patterns in the data.

As humans, we can often see patterns in small datasets with a few parameters. For example, take this small set of data for students studying for this exam, as shown in Figure 2-1.

Student	Background	Hours Studied	Completed Labs	Score	Pass
Student A	Computer Science	5	No	500	No
Student B	Computer Science	6	Yes	600	No
Student C	Mathematics	8	Yes	650	No
Student D	History	10	No	623	No
Student E	Computer Science	12	Yes	733	Yes
Student F	Mathematics	15	No	697	No
Student G	Mathematics	18	No	727	Yes
Student H	Computer Science	20	Yes	850	Yes
Student I	History	20	Yes	715	Yes
Student J	English	25	No	780	Yes
Student K	English	30	No	767	Yes

FIGURE 2-1 Sample data

You can probably see that there is a pattern that shows studying more hours leads to a higher exam score and passing the exam. However, can you see a pattern between the students' academic backgrounds and whether they pass or fail, and can you answer the question of how much does completing the labs affect their score? What if you were to have more information about the student, and what if there were many more records of data? This is where machine learning can help.

> **This skill covers how to:**
> - Understand machine learning model types
> - Describe regression models
> - Describe classification models
> - Describe clustering models

Understand machine learning model types

The amount of data created by businesses, people, their devices, and applications in ordinary daily life has grown exponentially and will grow even more as sensors are embedded into machinery in factories and in our devices and our homes. This volume of data is such that we can leverage it to improve the way we make decisions and how we operate.

Microsoft runs a competition for students called the Imagine Cup (https://imaginecup.microsoft.com). In the latest competition, students were asked to design solutions using AI to tackle global problems. As a judge, I evaluated the submissions, and the breadth and creativity of the proposals were astounding. We have not yet understood all the ways that machine learning can make a difference in our lives.

When you decide that you want to use machine learning, one of the first things is to decide what type of learning you will use in your model. The type of learning determines how your model will use data to determine its outcome:

- Supervised
- Unsupervised
- Reinforcement

Supervised learning

In *supervised learning*, the existing data contains the desired outcome. In machine learning, we say that the data contains a label. The labeled value is the output we want our model to determine for new data. A label can either be a value or a distinct category.

The other data that is supplied and that is used as inputs to the model are called features. A supervised learning model uses the features and label to train the model to fit the label to the features. After the model is trained, supplying the model with the features for new data will predict the value, or category, for the label.

You use supervised learning where you already have existing data that contains both the features and the label.

Unsupervised learning

In *unsupervised learning*, we do not have the outcome or label in the data. We use machine learning to determine the structure of the data and to look for commonalities or similarities in the data. Unsupervised learning separates the data based on the features.

You use unsupervised learning where you are trying to discover something about your data that you do not already know.

Reinforcement learning

Reinforcement learning uses feedback to improve the outcomes from the machine learning model. Reinforcement learning does not have labeled data.

Reinforcement learning uses a computer program, an agent, to determine if the outcome is optimal or not and feeds that back into the model so it can learn from itself.

Reinforcement learning is used, for example, in building a model to play chess and is commonly used in robotics.

Describe regression models

You will have probably used regression in school to draw a best fit line through a series of data points on a graph. Using the data from Figure 2-1, the hours studied are plotted against the exam scores, as shown in Figure 2-2.

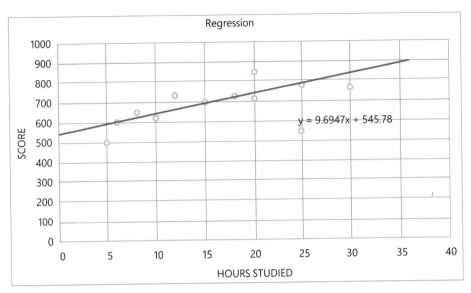

FIGURE 2-2 Regression graph

Regression is an example of supervised machine learning where the features (in this case, the hours studied) and the label (the exam score) are known and are both used to make the model fit the features to the label.

This graph is a very simple example of linear regression with just one feature. Regression models in machine learning can have many features. There are regression algorithms other than a simple linear regression that can be used.

EXAM TIP

For this exam, you do not need to know about the different algorithms, but you must be able to differentiate between the different learning models, regression, classification, and clustering.

Regression is used to predict a numeric value using a formula that is derived from historic data. Regression predicts continuous values, not distinct categories. In Figure 2-2, the formula that has been generated is y = 9.6947x + 545.78, which implies that every hour of studying increases the exam score by almost 10 points. We can use the model and ask the question how many hours a student should study to pass the exam (Microsoft exams require a score of 700 to pass). For 16 hours of studying, our model predicts a score of 700, a pass.

However, this is where we need to start considering how our data can affect the model. If we have another result where a student has studied for 30 hours and scored 650, the regression formula changes to y = 6.7243x + 579.49, as shown in Figure 2-3.

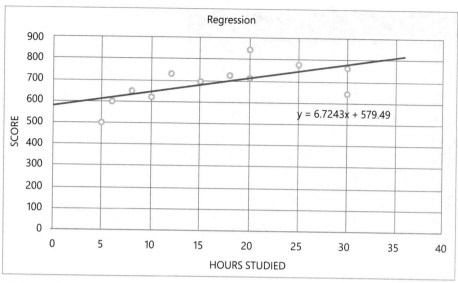

FIGURE 2-3 Regression graph with additional data

With this change to our model, we now need 18 hours of studying to pass the exam. In machine learning, one of the major concerns is how data can bias our model; we will discuss bias later in this chapter.

Describe classification models

Classification machine learning models are used to predict mutually exclusive categories, or classes. Classification involves learning using labels to classify data and is an example of supervised machine learning.

Classification is used to make predictions where we do not require continuous values but need distinct categories, such as Pass or Fail.

Using the same data from Figure 2-3, we could build and train a classification model to use the hours studied to predict whether a student passes the exam or not. Using this data, a simple two-class model will likely predict that studying for less than 18 hours will fail and 18 hours or more will pass.

In a classification model, we can compare the actual labels with the prediction from the model, as shown in the table in Figure 2-4.

Student	Hours Studied	Pass/Fail		Result
		Actual	Model	
Student A	5	No	No	True Negative
Student B	6	No	No	True Negative
Student C	8	No	No	True Negative
Student D	10	No	No	True Negative
Student E	12	Yes	No	False Negative
Student F	15	No	No	True Negative
Student G	18	Yes	Yes	True Positive
Student H	20	Yes	Yes	True Positive
Student I	20	Yes	Yes	True Positive
Student J	25	Yes	Yes	True Positive
Student K	30	Yes	Yes	True Positive
Student L	30	No	Yes	False Positive

FIGURE 2-4 Classification model

We can see that the classification model correctly predicts all but two of the results. If the model predicts a pass and the actual is a pass, this is a true positive. If the model predicts a fail and the actual is a fail, this is a true negative.

In a classification model, we are interested where the model gets it wrong. For student L, the model predicts a pass, but the actual result was a fail—this is a false positive. Student E actually passed, but the model predicted that the student will fail—this is a false negative.

Describe clustering models

Clustering machine models learn by discovering similarities, patterns, and relationships in the data without the data being labeled. *Clustering* is an example of unsupervised learning where the model attempts to discover structure from the data or tell us something about the data that we didn't know.

Clustering analyzes unlabeled data to find similarities in data points and groups them together into clusters. A clustering algorithm could be used, for example, to segment customers into multiple groups based on similarities in the customer's details and history.

A clustering model predicts mutually exclusive categories, or classes. K-means clustering is a common clustering model where K is the number of distinct clusters you want the model to group the data by. The way clustering works is to calculate the distance between the data point and the center of the cluster and then to minimize the distance of each data point to the center of its cluster.

Let's use our sample data but assume no one has taken the exam yet, so we do not have the scores or pass/fail. We have unlabeled data. Let's see if there is a relationship between the background of the students and the hours studied. We can plot these as shown in Figure 2-5.

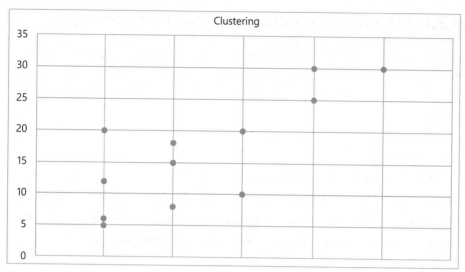

FIGURE 2-5 Clustering data

If we were to create a clustering model with K=3, then it might group the data into the three clusters—A, B, and C—as shown in Figure 2-6.

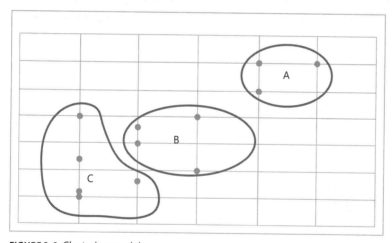

FIGURE 2-6 Clustering model

A common example of a clustering model is the recommender model. This is the model that was shown in Figure 1-1 for a company that wants to provide recommendations to its users by generating personalized targeted recommendations. A recommender model looks for similarities between customers. For example, a video streaming service knows which movies customers watch and can group customers by the types of movies they watch. A customer can then be shown other movies watched by other customers which are similar to them based on their viewing history.

Skill 2.2: Describe core machine learning concepts

Machine learning has several common concepts that apply when building machine learning models. These concepts apply no matter which tools, languages, or frameworks that you use. This section explains the fundamental concepts and processes involved in building machine learning models.

> **This skill covers how to:**
> - Understand the machine learning workflow
> - Identify the features and labels in a dataset for machine learning
> - Describe how training and validation datasets are used in machine learning
> - Describe how machine learning algorithms are used for model training
> - Select and interpret model evaluation metrics

Understand the machine learning workflow

Building a machine learning model follows the process outlined in Figure 2-7. It is important to note that building a model is an iterative process where the model is evaluated and refined.

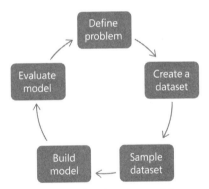

FIGURE 2-7 Machine learning workflow

First, you define the problem. This means translating the business problem into a machine learning problem statement. For example, if you are asked to understand how groups of customers behave, you would transform that as create a clustering model using customer data.

In the example used in this chapter, we want to discover how much activity a student needs to undertake to pass the exam. So far, we have kept this simple just by looking at the hours studied, but we have been asked to look at other factors such as whether they have completed the labs and their choice of degree subject. We could transform these into the following problem statements:

- Create a regression model to predict a student's score for the exam using their degree subject and their exam preparation activities.

- Create a classification model to predict if a student will pass the exam using their degree subject and their exam preparation activities.

Identify the features and labels in a dataset for machine learning

The next step in the machine learning workflow is to create a dataset. Data is the most important asset you have as you use data to train your model. If your data is incomplete or inaccurate, then it will have a major impact on how well your model performs.

You must first collect your data. This can mean extracting data from multiple systems, transforming, cleansing, and importing the data.

EXAM TIP

How to extract and transform data is outside the scope of this exam.

We will start with the same dataset we used earlier in this chapter with some additional exam results, as shown in the table in Figure 2-8.

Student	Background	Hours Studied	Completed Labs	Score	Pass
Student A	Computer Science	5	No	500	No
Student B	Computer Science	6	Yes	600	No
Student C	Mathematics	8	Yes	650	No
Student D	History	10	No	623	No
Student E	Computer Science	12	Yes	733	Yes
Student F	Mathematics	15	No	697	No
Student G	Mathematics	18	No	727	Yes
Student H	Computer Science	20	Yes	850	Yes
Student I	History	20	Yes	715	Yes
Student J	English	25	No	780	Yes
Student K	English	30	No	767	Yes
Student L	Psychology	30	No	650	No
Student M	Computer Science	20	No	727	Yes
Student N	Mathematics	17	Yes	600	No

FIGURE 2-8 Dataset

Identify labels

If you are using supervised training—for example, a regression or a classification model—then you need to select the label(s) from your dataset. Labels are the columns in the dataset that the model predicts.

For a regression model, the Score column is the label you would choose, as this is a numeric value. Regression models are used to predict a range of values.

For a classification model, the Pass column is the label you would choose as this column has distinct values. Classification models are used to predict from a list of distinct categories.

Feature selection

A *feature* is a column in your dataset. You use features to train the model to predict the outcome. Features are used to train the model to fit the label. After training the model, you can supply new data containing the same features, and the model will predict the value for the column you have selected as the label.

The possible features in our dataset are the following:

- Background
- Hours Studied
- Completed Labs

In the real world, you will have other possible features to choose from.

Feature selection is the process of selecting a subset of relevant features to use when building and training the model. Feature selection restricts the data to the most valuable inputs, reducing noise and improving training performance.

Feature engineering

Feature engineering is the process of creating new features from raw data to increase the predictive power of the machine learning model. Engineered features capture additional information that is not available in the original feature set.

Examples of feature engineering are as follows:

- Aggregating data
- Calculating a moving average
- Calculating the difference over time
- Converting text into a numeric value
- Grouping data

Models train better with numeric data rather than text strings. In some circumstances, data that visually appears to be numeric may be held as text strings, and you need to parse and convert the data type into a numeric value.

In our dataset, the background column, the degree subject names for our students, may not perform well when we evaluate our model. One option might be to classify the degree subjects into humanities and sciences and then to convert to a Boolean value, such as IsScienceSubject, with values of 1 for True and 0 for False.

Bias

Bias in machine learning is the impact of erroneous assumptions that our model makes about our data. Machine learning models depend on the quality, objectivity, and quantity of data used to train it. Faulty, incomplete, or prejudicial data can result in a poorly performing model.

In Chapter 1, we introduced the Fairness principle and how an AI model should be concerned with how data influences the model's prediction to help eliminate bias. You should therefore be conscious of the provenance of the data you are using in your model. You should evaluate the bias that might be introduced by the data you have selected.

A common issue is that the algorithm is unable to learn the true signal from the data, and instead, noise in the data can overly influence the model. An example from computer vision is where the army attempted to build a model that was able to find enemy tanks in photographs of landscapes. The model was built with many different photographs with and without tanks in them. The model performed well in testing and evaluation, but when deployed, the model was unable to find tanks. Eventually, it was realized that all pictures of tanks were taken on cloudy days, and all pictures without tanks were taken on sunny days. They had built a model that identifies whether a photograph was of a sunny or a cloudy day; the noise of the sunlight biased the model. The problem of bias was resolved by adding additional photographs into the dataset with varying degrees of cloud cover.

It can be tempting to select all columns as features for your model. You may then find when you evaluate the model that one column significantly biases the model, with the model effectively ignoring the other columns. You should consider removing that column as a feature if it is irrelevant.

Normalization

A common cause of bias in a model is caused by data in numeric features having different ranges of values. Machine learning algorithms tend to be influenced by the size of values, so if one feature ranges in values between 1 and 10 and another feature between 1 and 100, the latter column will bias the model toward that feature.

You mitigate possible bias by normalizing the numeric features, so they are on the same numeric scale.

After feature selection, feature engineering, and normalization, our dataset might appear as in the table in Figure 2-9.

ID	Feature	Feature	Feature	Label	Label
Student	ISScienceSubject	Hours Studied	Completed Labs	Score	Pass
Student A	1	0.1667	0	500	0
Student B	1	0.2000	1	600	0
Student C	1	0.2667	1	650	0
Student D	0	0.3333	0	623	0
Student E	1	0.4000	1	733	1
Student F	1	0.5000	0	697	0
Student G	1	0.6000	0	727	1
Student H	1	0.6667	1	850	1
Student I	0	0.6667	1	715	1
Student J	0	0.8333	0	780	1
Student K	0	1.0000	0	767	1
Student L	0	1.0000	0	650	0
Student M	1	0.6667	0	727	1
Student N	1	0.5667	1	600	0

FIGURE 2-9 Normalized dataset

Describe how training and validation datasets are used in machine learning

After you have created your dataset, you need to create sample datasets for use in training and evaluating your model.

Typically, you split your dataset into two datasets when building a machine learning model:

- **Training** The training dataset is the sample of data used to train the model. It is the largest sample of data used when creating a machine learning model.

- **Testing** The testing, or validation, dataset is a second sample of data used to provide a validation of the model to see if the model can correctly predict, or classify, using data not seen before.

A common ratio between training and validation data volumes is 70:30, but you may vary this ratio depending on your needs and size of your data.

You need to be careful when splitting the data. If you simply take the first set of rows, then you may bias your data by date created or however the data is sorted. You should randomize the selected data so that both training and testing datasets are representative of the entire dataset.

For example, we might split our dataset as shown in Figure 2-10.

Training

Student	ISScienceSubject	Hours Studied	Completed Labs	Score	Pass
Student A	1	0.1667	0	500	0
Student C	1	0.2667	1	650	0
Student D	0	0.3333	0	623	0
Student F	1	0.5000	0	697	0
Student G	1	0.6000	0	727	1
Student I	0	0.6667	1	715	1
Student J	0	0.8333	0	780	1
Student L	0	1.0000	0	650	0
Student M	1	0.6667	0	727	1

Testing

Student	ISScienceSubject	Hours Studied	Completed Labs	Score	Pass
Student B	1	0.2000	1	600	0
Student E	1	0.4000	1	733	1
Student H	1	0.6667	1	850	1
Student K	0	1.0000	0	767	1
Student N	1	0.9667	1	600	0

ID	Feature	Feature	Feature	Label	Label
Student	ISScienceSubject	Hours Studied	Completed Labs	Score	Pass
Student A	1	0.1667	0	500	0
Student B	1	0.2000	1	600	0
Student C	1	0.2667	0	650	0
Student D	0	0.3333	0	623	0
Student E	1	0.4000	1	733	1
Student F	1	0.5000	0	697	0
Student G	1	0.6000	0	727	1
Student H	1	0.6667	1	850	1
Student I	0	0.6667	1	715	1
Student J	0	0.8333	0	780	1
Student K	0	1.0000	0	767	1
Student L	0	1.0000	0	650	0
Student M	1	0.6667	0	727	1
Student N	1	0.9667	1	600	0

FIGURE 2-10 Training and testing datasets

Describe how machine learning algorithms are used for model training

A machine learning model learns the relationships between the features and the label in the training dataset.

It is at this point that you select the algorithm to train the model with.

> **NOTE ALGORITHMS**
>
> For this exam, you do not need to know about algorithms or which algorithm should be used for which machine learning problem. If you want to find out more about algorithms, see https://aka.ms/mlcheatsheet.

The algorithm finds patterns and relationships in the training data that map the input data features to the label that you want to predict. The algorithm outputs a machine learning model that captures these patterns.

Training a model can take a significant amount of time and processing power. The cloud has enabled data scientists to use the scalability of the cloud to build models more quickly and with more data than can be achieved with on-premises hardware.

After training, you use the model to predict the label based on its features. You provide the model with new input containing the features (Hours Studied, Completed Labs) and the model will return the predicted label (Score or Pass) for that student.

Select and interpret model evaluation metrics

After a model has been trained, you need to evaluate how well the model has performed. First, you score the model using the data in the testing dataset that was split earlier from the dataset. This data has not been seen by the model, as it was not used to build the model.

To evaluate the model, you compare the prediction values for the label with the known actual values to obtain a measure of the amount of error. You then create metrics to help gauge the performance of the model and explore the results.

There are different ways to measure and evaluate regression, classification, and clustering models.

Evaluate regression models

When evaluating a regression model, you estimate the amount of error in the predicted values.

To determine the amount of error in a regression model, you measure the difference between the actual values you have for the label and the predicted values for the label. These are known as the residual values. A way to represent the amount of error is to draw a line from each data point perpendicular to the best fit line, as shown in Figure 2-11.

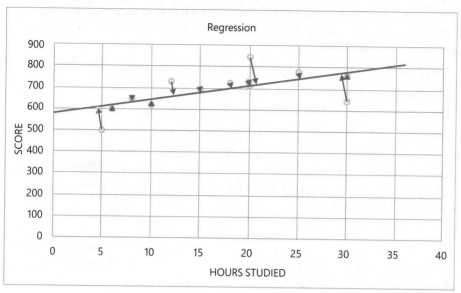

FIGURE 2-11 Regression errors

The length of the lines indicates the size of residual values in the model. A model is considered to fit the data well if the difference between actual and predicted values is small.

The following metrics can be used when evaluating regression models:

- **Mean absolute error (MAE)**   Measures how close the predictions are to the actual values; lower is better.

- **Root mean squared error (RMSE)**   The square root of the average squared distance between the actual and the predicted values; lower is better.

- **Relative absolute error (RAE)**   Relative absolute difference between expected and actual values; lower is better.

- **Relative squared error (RSE)**   The total squared error of the predicted values by dividing by the total squared error of the actual values; lower is better.

- **Mean Zero One Error (MZOE)**   If the prediction was correct or not with values 0 or 1.

- **Coefficient of determination (R2 or R-squared)**   A measure of the variance from the mean in its predictions; the closer to 1, the better the model is performing.

We will see later that Azure Machine Learning calculates these metrics for us.

Evaluate classification models

In a classification model with distinct categories predicted, we are interested where the model gets it right or gets it wrong.

A common way to represent how a classification model is right or wrong is to create a confusion matrix. In a confusion matrix, the numbers of true positives, true negatives, false positives, and false negatives are shown:

- **True Positive**   The model predicted true, and the actual is true.
- **True Negative**   The model predicted false, and the actual is false.
- **False Positive**   The model predicted true, and the actual is false.
- **False Negative**   The model predicted negative, and the actual is true.

The total number of true positives is shown in the top-left corner, and the total number of true negatives is shown in the bottom-right corner. The total number of false positives is shown in the top-right corner, and the total number of false negatives is shown in the bottom-left corner, as shown in Figure 2-12.

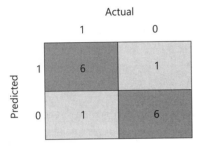

FIGURE 2-12 Confusion matrix

> **NOTE   CONFUSION MATRIX**
>
> Confusion matrixes are not always shown in the same way by different authors and tools. For instance, the actual and predicted headings may be swapped, and the 1 and 0 can be reversed.

From the values in the confusion matrix, you can calculate metrics to measure the performance of the model:

- **Accuracy**   The number of true positives and true negatives; the total of correct predictions, divided by the total number of predictions.
- **Precision**   The number of true positives divided by the sum of the number of true positives and false positives.
- **Recall**   The number of true positives divided by the sum of the number of true positives and false negatives.
- **F-score**   Combines precision and recall as a weighted mean value.
- **Area Under Curve (AUC)**   A measure of true positive rate over true negative rate.

All these metrics are scored between 0 and 1, with closer to 1 being better.

We will see later that Azure Machine Learning generates the confusion matric and calculates these metrics for us.

Evaluate clustering models

Clustering models are created by minimizing the distance of a data point to the center point of its cluster.

The Average Distance to Cluster Center metric is used when evaluating clustering models and is a measure of how focused the clusters are. The lower the value, the better.

Skill 2.3: Identify core tasks in creating a machine learning solution

Azure provides several different tools and services to build and manage machine learning models. While the tools vary, many of the tasks involved are very similar. This section describes how you use Azure Machine Learning to build and deploy machine learning models.

This skill covers how to:
- Understand machine learning on Azure
- Understand Azure Machine Learning studio
- Describe data ingestion and preparation
- Describe feature selection and engineering
- Describe model training and evaluation
- Describe model deployment and management

Understand machine learning on Azure

Azure provides many different ways to create and use Artificial Intelligence models. You can use the prebuilt models in Azure Cognitive Services, or you can build and deploy your own models with Azure Machine Learning services.

Machine learning on Azure

Microsoft provides a number of services created by Microsoft for machine learning and supports a wider set of open source and third-party services for data science and Artificial Intelligence that you can use within Azure for your own AI solutions.

The Azure Marketplace contains services and solutions for machine learning from both Microsoft and its partners, as shown in Figure 2-13.

If you are used to tools such as PyCharm or Jupyter notebooks, you can use these within Azure and leverage other Azure services such as compute and storage.

If you are used to frameworks such as PyTorch, Scikit-Learn, TensorFlow, or ONNX, you can use these frameworks within Azure.

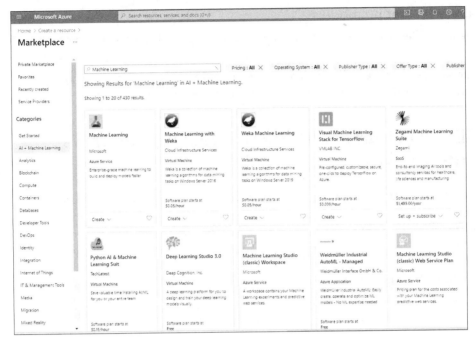

FIGURE 2-13 Azure Marketplace

If you are used to using Apache Spark, you can use Azure Databricks, Microsoft's implementation of Apache Spark that integrates tightly with other Azure services.

If you are used to Microsoft SQL Server machine learning, you can use an Azure Data Science virtual machine (DSVM), which comes with ML tools and R and Python installed.

You can also configure and use your own virtual machine configured using the tools and services that you may prefer.

As there are many different options available, we will focus on the native Azure services provided by Microsoft.

Azure Machine Learning workspace

To use Azure Machine Learning services, you first need access to an Azure subscription. An Azure subscription defines how you are billed for using Azure resources.

You then need to create an Azure Machine Learning workspace. An Azure ML workspace is a container for all of your resources used in building and deploying models, data, experiments, compute, and web services.

The purpose of a Machine Learning workspace is to make the building, training, and deployment of machine learning models easier, reducing the steps required and integrating storage and compute all within a secure environment.

Figure 2-14 shows the service description for Azure Machine Learning workspace.

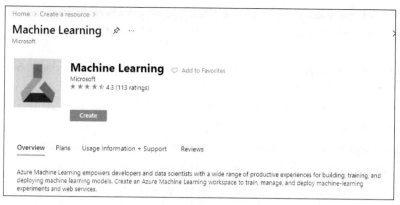

FIGURE 2-14 Machine Learning workspace service description

After clicking on the Create button, the Create Machine Learning workspace pane opens, as shown in Figure 2-15.

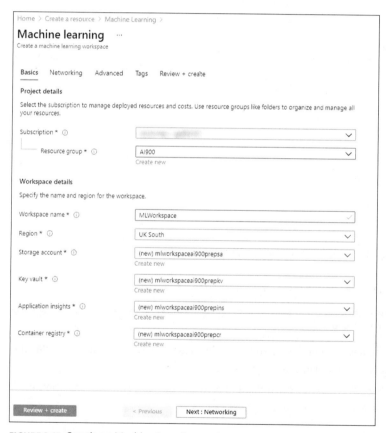

FIGURE 2-15 Creating a Machine Learning workspace resource

You will need to select the subscription, resource group, and region where the resource is to be deployed. You will then need to create a unique name for the workspace. There are four related Azure services:

- **Storage account**   The default datastore for the workspace for data used to train models as well as files used and generated by the workspace.

- **Key vault**   Securely stores secrets such as authentication keys and credentials that are used by the workspace.

- **Application insights**   Stores monitoring information for your deployed models.

- **Container registry**   Stores Docker images used in training and deployments.

You can either select existing resources or create new resources for these related services.

Clicking on Review + create will validate the options. You then click on Create to create the resource. The resource will be deployed after a few minutes.

Once your resource has been created, you can view the resources associated with the workspace, as shown in Figure 2-16.

FIGURE 2-16 Azure resources for a Machine Learning workspace

You can create a Machine Learning workspace using the CLI as follows:

```
az ml workspace create -workspace_name <unique name> --resource-group <resource
group name> --location <region>
```

To access the workspace, you need to open the workspace in the portal. This will display the details of the workspace, as shown in Figure 2-17.

You can use Role-Based Access Control (RBAC) to give users permission to access the workspace and its resources, and to create and run experiments.

FIGURE 2-17 Machine Learning workspace resource

An Azure Machine Learning workspace is used to manage your machine learning assets:

- **Compute** The virtual machines and Docker containers used for development, training, and deployment of models.
- **Datasets** The data used for experimentation and training models.
- **Pipelines** The connected steps for a machine learning model. A pipeline can contain the data ingestion, training, scoring, and evaluation steps.
- **Experiments** The results for each run of a pipeline, including metrics and outputs.
- **Models** The trained models.
- **Endpoints** The web services for deployed models.

Before you can start working with your workspace, you need to assign compute resources to the workspace. These are referred to as compute targets:

- **Compute instance** A development virtual machine used to process data and build your model.
- **Compute cluster** A cluster of scalable virtual machines for training your model and running experiments.
- **Inference cluster** Azure Kubernetes Service (AKS) cluster for running a deployed model to perform predictions.
- **Attached compute** Existing Azure virtual machines or other ML services, such as Azure Databricks.

> **NOTE   COMPUTE**
>
> You need compute targets to run machine learning workloads in the cloud instead of on your local computer. You can perform model development on local compute with low volumes of data using Visual Studio Code.

The high-level process for an Azure Machine Learning workspace is shown in Figure 2-18.

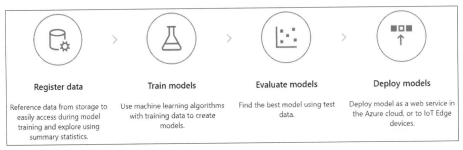

Register data	Train models	Evaluate models	Deploy models
Reference data from storage to easily access during model training and explore using summary statistics.	Use machine learning algorithms with training data to create models.	Find the best model using test data.	Deploy model as a web service in the Azure cloud, or to IoT Edge devices.

FIGURE 2-18 Machine Learning workspace process

You need to manage the data needed to build machine learning solutions. You can then build and train your model. All the outputs of each experiment are stored in the workspace to allow you to evaluate the model. When you are content that your model performs well, you publish your model as a web service that can be accessed via an HTTP endpoint.

Azure Machine Learning workspaces are tightly integrated with the Visual Studio Code IDE. Using Visual Studio Code you can build, train, and deploy machine learning models with Azure Machine Learning. Visual Studio Code supports creating machine learning models with .NET and R languages, as well as with Python and Jupyter notebooks. Figure 2-19 shows the Visual Studio Code connected to the Azure Machine Learning workspace and running Python code in a Jupyter notebook.

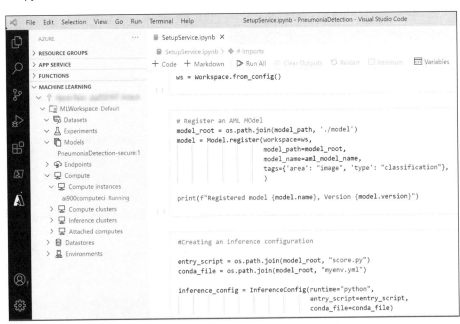

FIGURE 2-19 Visual Studio Code

EXAM TIP

For this exam, you do not need to know how to write code for machine learning, but you do need to know about the different languages and tools for building models.

Understand Azure Machine Learning studio

In the Machine Learning workspace resource, you will see a button called Launch studio. Clicking on this button will open the Machine Learning studio at https://ml.azure.com/, as shown in Figure 2-20.

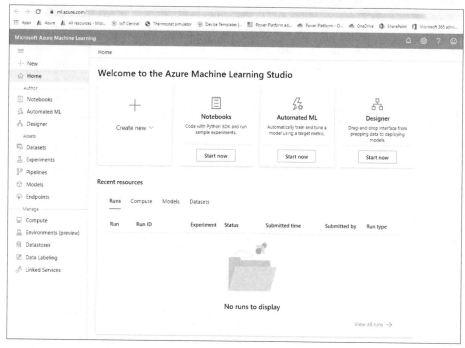

FIGURE 2-20 Azure Machine Learning studio

Machine Learning studio allows you to create and manage the assets in your Machine Learning workspace using a graphical user interface.

Author

Azure Machine Learning studio supports both no-code and code-first experiences. You can build, train, and run machine learning models with Automated Machine Learning, Notebooks, and a Visual drag-and-drop designer.

Azure Machine Learning studio supports the use of Jupyter notebooks that use the Python SDK to create and run machine learning models.

Automated Machine Learning (AutoML) is a no-code tool that performs many of the steps required to build and train a model automatically, reducing the need for deep machine learning skills and domain knowledge. You just select the training data and the required model type, and AutoML determines the best algorithm to use and trains the model.

The Designer (drag-and-drop ML) is a no-code tool that allows you to build pipelines for data preparation and model creation.

The AutoML and Designer tools are explained in Skill 2.4 later in this chapter.

Compute

Before you can start ingesting data or building a model, you must first assign a compute instance. A *compute instance* is a configured development virtual machine environment for machine learning. A compute instance is used as a compute target for authoring and training models for development and testing purposes.

Clicking on Compute in the left-hand navigation pane of Azure Machine Learning studio displays the Compute options, as shown in Figure 2-21.

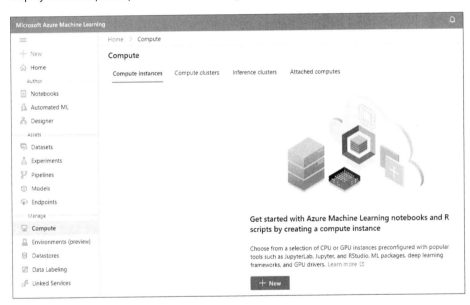

FIGURE 2-21 Machine Learning studio compute

After clicking on the + New button, the Create compute instance pane opens, as shown in Figure 2-22.

You will need to provide a unique name for the instance; select the machine type and size. You then click on Create to create the virtual machine. The virtual machine will be created and started after a few minutes. You will be able to see the state of the virtual machine, as shown in Figure 2-23.

FIGURE 2-22 Create a compute instance

FIGURE 2-23 Compute instances

> **NOTE   STOP COMPUTE INSTANCES WHEN NOT BEING USED**
>
> The virtual machine used for the compute instance does not shut down automatically. When not building machine learning models, you should stop the virtual machines under compute instances to reduce Azure spend. It is easy to start the virtual machine again when you next need it.

You can stop the virtual machine used for the compute instance by clicking on the stop button, as shown in Figure 2-24.

FIGURE 2-24 Compute instance

Describe data ingestion and preparation

To train a model, you need to supply data for training and testing. You are going to need to either import your own data into the Machine Learning workspace or link to existing datastores used by other applications.

Ingestion

Each Machine Learning workspace has two built-in datastores: one for data used for training and evaluating models and another for files used by machine learning, such as logs and output files.

Figure 2-25 shows the built-in datastores in the Machine Learning workspace.

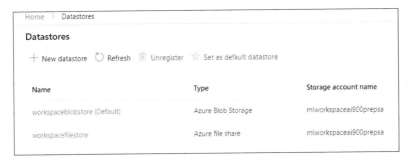

FIGURE 2-25 Datastores

When you click on the + New datastore button, you can add in the following existing datastores:

- Azure Blob Storage
- Azure file share

- Azure Data Lake Gen 1
- Azure Data Lake Gen 2
- Azure SQL database
- Azure PostgreSQL
- Azure MySQL database

If you have existing data in Azure SQL database, you supply the details of the Azure SQL database, as shown in Figure 2-26.

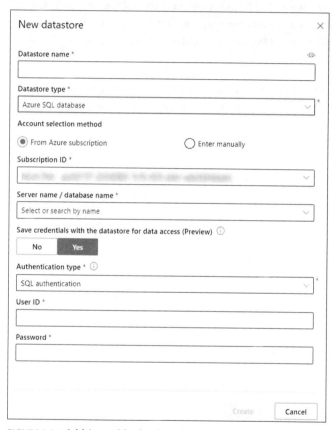

FIGURE 2-26 Add Azure SQL database

If you want to import your data into the Azure Machine Learning workspace, you register datasets using Machine Learning studio. You can create a dataset from:

- Files uploaded from your local computer
- A datastore associated with the workspace
- Files accessed via an HTTP URL
- Open datasets

When you import data, you must define the dataset type as either tabular or file:

- **Tabular** Files containing data in a tabular format. You can create a tabular dataset from CSV, TSV, Parquet, JSON files, and from the output of an SQL query.

- **File** A collection of file references in datastores or public URLs. A file dataset references single or multiple files.

> **NOTE CREATING DATASETS**
>
> You can create a dataset from the output of a SQL query but not from a SQL query itself. You can create a dataset from files in an Azure Blob container but not from an Azure Blob container itself. You can create a dataset from files in a folder but not from a folder itself.

The student data we referenced earlier in this chapter is held in a CSV file on a local computer. After clicking on + Create dataset, the Create dataset from the local files wizard is displayed, as shown in Figure 2-27.

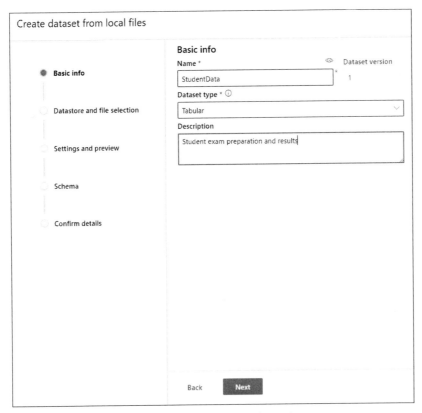

FIGURE 2-27 Create a dataset from the local files wizard, step 1

You must enter the name of the dataset, select the dataset type as either Tabular or File. Clicking on Next displays the next step in the wizard, as shown in Figure 2-28.

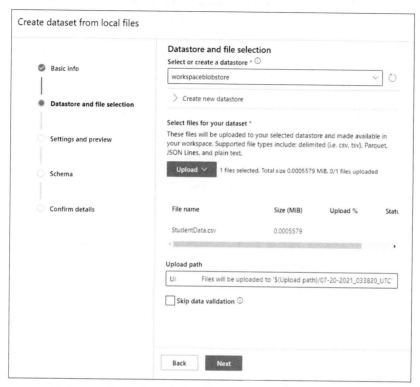

FIGURE 2-28 Create a dataset from the local files wizard, step 2

You select the datastore where the data will be imported into. This will normally be the built-in blob datastore, but you can add your own datastore if required. You can then upload a single file or select an entire folder of files to upload. Clicking on Next will parse the selected file(s) and display the next step in the wizard, as shown in Figure 2-29.

You can review the tabular data to ensure it has been parsed correctly. Clicking on Next displays the next step in the wizard, as shown in Figure 2-30.

You can exclude columns from being imported and correct any data type for each column. Clicking on Next displays the final step in the wizard, as shown in Figure 2-31.

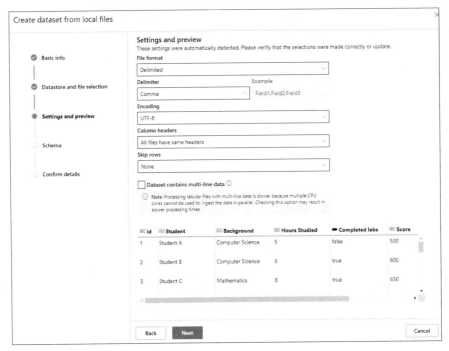

FIGURE 2-29 Create a dataset from the local files wizard, step 3

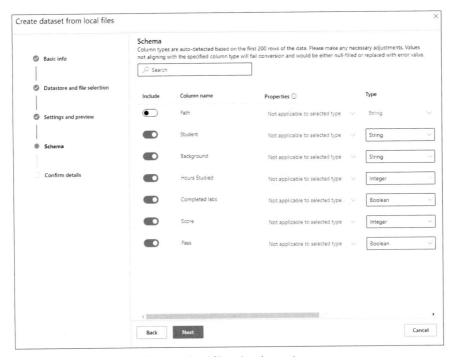

FIGURE 2-30 Create a dataset from the local files wizard, step 4

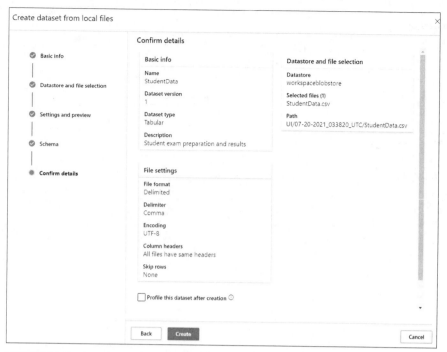

FIGURE 2-31 Create a dataset from the local files wizard, step 5

Clicking on Create will import the data and register the dataset, as shown in Figure 2-32.

FIGURE 2-32 Registered datasets

You can use publicly available data from URLs such as daily bike rental data that can be found at http://aka.ms/bike-rentals. You can import this dataset, as shown in Figure 2-33.

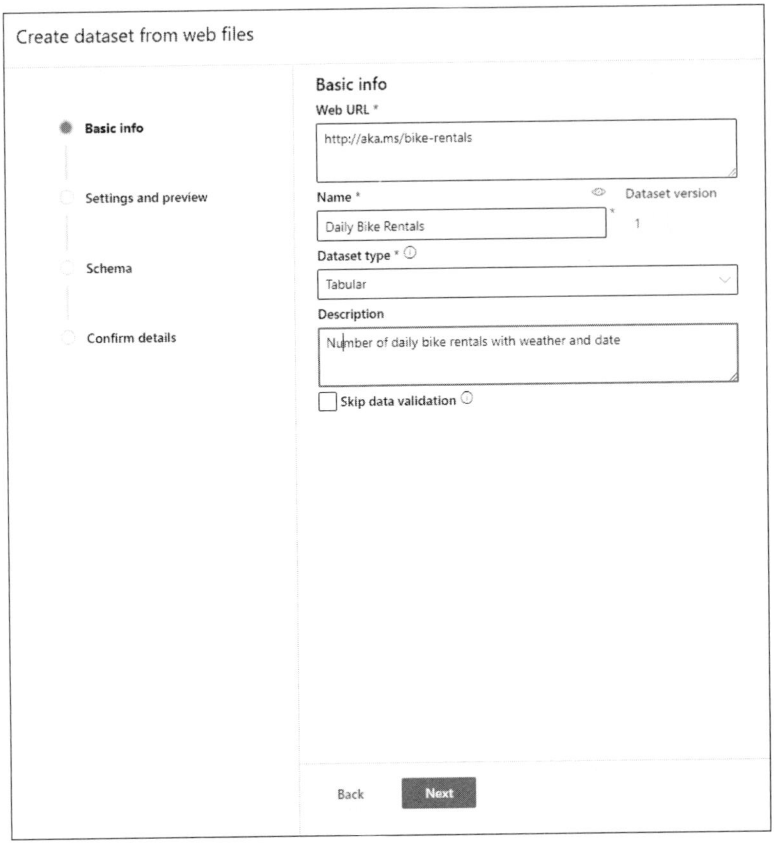

FIGURE 2-33 Create a dataset from the local files wizard, step 1

Azure Open datasets are curated datasets publicly available on Azure that you can import into your machine learning model, as shown in Figure 2-34.

You can simply add these datasets to your workspace. To find out more about these and other publicly available datasets, see https://docs.microsoft.com/azure/open-datasets/dataset-catalog.

> *NOTE* **SAMPLE DATASETS**
>
> There are a further 16 sample datasets available in the Azure Machine Learning designer tool (https://docs.microsoft.com/azure/machine-learning/samples-designer#datasets).

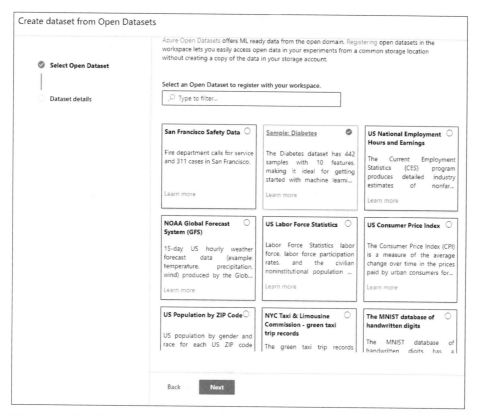

FIGURE 2-34 Open datasets

Preparation

Once you have ingested your data, you will need to prepare your data for training and testing models. A good place to start is to explore the profile of the data. In Machine Learning studio, you can generate and review the profile of your data, as shown in Figure 2-35.

The profile will inform you of issues with your data that require transformation and cleansing.

There are many actions you can perform to transform your dataset, including the following:

- **Normalization** Adjusting the values in numeric columns so that all numeric values are on a common scale, normally between 0 and 1. A dataset that has features with different ranges can bias the model toward that feature.

- **Partitioning and sampling** A method for reducing the size of data while retaining the same ratio of values.

How you perform these actions will depend on the tool you choose to build and train your model.

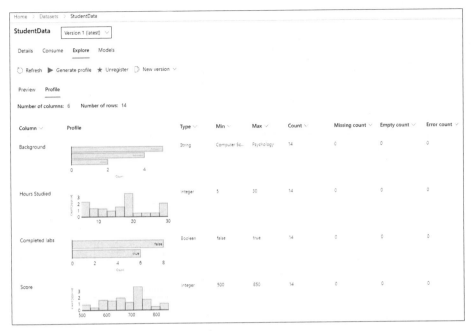

FIGURE 2-35 Dataset profile

Data that is incomplete can cause issues when training your model. You can clean missing data by methods such as the following:

- Replacing missing values with an average or another value.
- Removing empty (or sparsely populated) rows.

Describe feature selection and engineering

Once the data has been prepared, the next step is to choose the features that you will use to train the model. You can select features from the dataset, but it may be necessary to engineer new features.

Feature selection

Feature selection is the process of selecting a subset of the columns in the dataset features to exclude features that are not relevant to the machine learning problem that we are trying to resolve. Feature selection restricts the data to the most valuable inputs, reducing noise and improving training performance.

Feature selection has two main purposes:

- Increase the model's ability to classify data accurately by eliminating features that are irrelevant, redundant, or highly correlated.
- Increase the efficiency of the model training process.

If you can reduce the number of features without losing the variance and patterns in the data, the time taken to train the model is minimized. For instance, you can exclude features that are highly correlated with each other as this just adds redundancy to the processing.

Azure Machine Learning has a module for Filter-Based Feature Selection to assist in identifying features that are irrelevant. Azure Machine Learning applies statistical analysis to determine which columns are more predictive than the others and ranks the results. You can exclude the columns that have a poor predictive effect.

Feature engineering

Feature engineering is the process of creating new features from raw data to increase the predictive power of the machine learning model. Engineered features capture additional information that is not available in the original feature set. Examples of feature engineering are aggregating data, calculating a moving average, and calculating the difference over time.

It can be beneficial to aggregate data in the source data, reducing the amount of data imported and used to train the model.

In Azure Machine Learning, you can use modules such as feature hashing that use Cognitive Services to turn text into indices. For example, in our student data, we could apply feature hashing to convert the academic subject for each student into a numeric hash value.

Binning is an example of feature engineering where the data is segmented into groups of the same size. Binning is used when the distribution of values in the data is skewed. Binning transforms continuous numeric features into discrete categories.

A common example of feature engineering is around dates and times. You can convert dates and times to the relative number of days, hours, and minutes or take two datetime columns and creating the difference in minutes between. This might create a model that predicts more accurate outcomes.

Another similar example of feature engineering is to extract features from a single column, such as converting a date into the following data:

- Day of the week
- Day of the month
- Month
- Year
- Weekend or weekday
- Public holiday or working day

The daily bike rentals data shows how such features have been engineered.

Describe model training and evaluation

Azure Machine Learning provides several ways to train your models, from code-first solutions using the various SDKs to no-code tools.

There are different ways to train the model depending on which option you choose. You can either create a configuration script—for example, in Python—and then run a training job, or you can use *pipelines*, which are workflows containing reusable modules.

> **NOTE PIPELINES**
>
> Pipelines are more flexible and are not limited simply to training and can include other steps, such as data ingestion and preparation.

Compute cluster

Before you can train a model, you need to assign compute resources to your workspace. A compute cluster is used to train models with the Azure Machine Learning workspace. The cluster can also be used for generating predictions on large amounts of data in batch mode.

Clicking on Compute in the left-hand navigation pane displays the Compute options, as shown previously in Figure 2-21. Clicking the Compute clusters tab displays any existing cluster. After clicking on the + New button, the Create compute cluster pane opens, as shown in Figure 2-36.

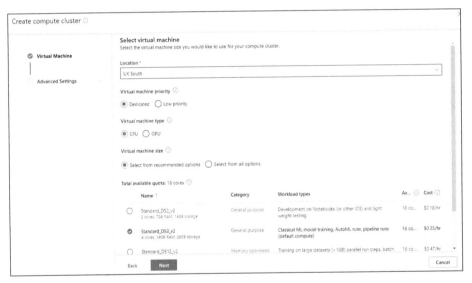

FIGURE 2-36 Create compute cluster

You will need to select the machine type and size. Clicking on Next displays the cluster settings pane, as shown in Figure 2-37.

You will need to provide a unique name for the cluster and specify the minimum and maximum number of nodes in the cluster. You then click on Create to create the cluster. The cluster will be created after a few minutes. You will be able to see the state of the cluster, as shown in Figure 2-38.

FIGURE 2-37 Create compute cluster settings

FIGURE 2-38 Compute clusters

The number of active nodes will scale up and down automatically based on the training you are performing in the workspace.

> **NOTE** **MINIMIZE COMPUTE CLUSTER NODES WHEN NOT BEING USED**
>
> The nodes in the compute cluster will stop automatically based on the idle time, which defaults to 30 minutes. When not training machine learning models, you should reduce the number of nodes to reduce Azure spend. It is easy to increase the number of nodes again when you next need them.

You can change the number of nodes used in the compute cluster by changing the minimum and maximum number of nodes, as shown in Figure 2-39.

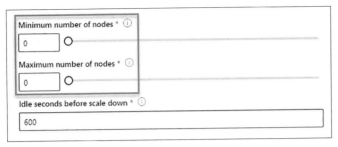

FIGURE 2-39 Compute cluster nodes

If you are not training models, you can set both numbers to zero.

Training

Training a model requires a combination of dataset, algorithm, and compute. Azure Machine Learning allows you to easily train a model, but in the real world, you need to run multiple experiments with different features and algorithms to build the best performing model.

Before training, you should have transformed and cleansed your dataset, selected features, performed any feature engineering required, and normalized the data. By properly preparing your dataset, you can improve the accuracy of the trained model.

Azure Machine Learning logs metrics for every experiment, and you can use these metrics to evaluate the model's performance.

Once you have deployed your model, training does not stop. You may get additional data, and you will need to train and evaluate the model. As was discussed earlier, building models is an iterative process. But it is not just iterative—it is an ongoing process. With Azure Machine Learning, you can create new versions of your model and then deploy a version to replace the existing deployed model. You can also revert to an older version of the model if the version you have deployed does not perform well with new data.

Many algorithms have parameters, known as *hyperparameters*, that you can set. Hyperparameters control how model training is done, which can have a significant impact on model accuracy. Azure Machine Learning has a module that allows for tuning hyperparameters by iterating multiple times with combinations of parameters to find the best fit model

With the K-means clustering algorithm, you can adjust the K, which is the target number of clusters you want the model to find. Increasing K increases the compute time and cost.

Scoring

Azure Machine Learning contains a module that can split data into training and testing datasets. Once the model has been trained, you use the testing dataset to score the model.

The testing dataset contains data that was not used to train the model—data that is new to the model. You use the trained model to generate predictions for each row in the testing dataset. Azure Machine Learning enables visualization of the results from scoring, as shown in

Figure 2-40 for a regression model using our student dataset and using the hours studied as a single feature and the score as the label.

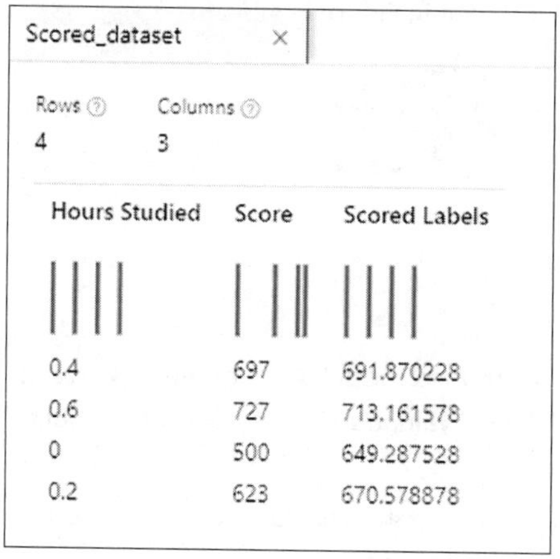

Scored_dataset

Rows 4 Columns 3

Hours Studied	Score	Scored Labels
0.4	697	691.870228
0.6	727	713.161578
0	500	649.287528
0.2	623	670.578878

FIGURE 2-40 Score results for regression

In the results, you can see that the prediction (the scored label) for the first two rows is close to the actual score, but the other two rows are showing higher residual errors. The third row has a predicted score of 649, but the actual score was 500; the fourth row has a predicted score of 670, but the actual score was 623.

Figure 2-41 shows the scores for a classification model using our student dataset and using the hours studied and completed labs as features and pass as the label.

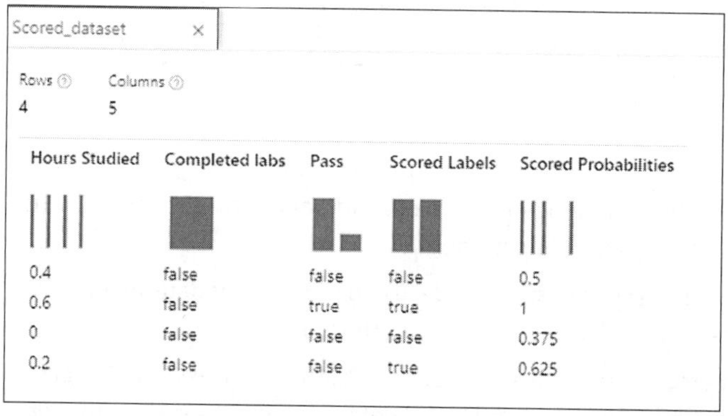

Scored_dataset

Rows 4 Columns 5

Hours Studied	Completed labs	Pass	Scored Labels	Scored Probabilities
0.4	false	false	false	0.5
0.6	false	true	true	1
0	false	false	false	0.375
0.2	false	false	true	0.625

FIGURE 2-41 Score results for classification

In the results, you can see that the prediction (the scored label) for the first three rows is correct. The first row is a true negative, with the actual and prediction both false with a probability of 50%. The second row is a true positive, with the actual and prediction both true with a probability of 100%. The third row is a true negative, with the actual and prediction both false, but with a probability of only 37.5%. The fourth row is a false positive, with the actual being a fail but the model predicting a pass.

Once you have scored your model, you use the scores to generate metrics to evaluate the model's performance and how good the predictions of the model are.

The sequence of the tasks when building a model is shown in Figure 2-42.

FIGURE 2-42 Sequence of model-building tasks

Evaluation

Evaluation is the process of measuring the accuracy of a trained model. A set of metrics is used to measure how accurate the predictions of the model are. Evaluation is a key part of the building of your model.

Azure Machine Learning generates metrics for each experiment. You can view these metrics to evaluate your model's performance (as shown previously in Figure 2-42) for a regression model using our student dataset, with the hours studied as a single feature and the score as the label, as shown in Figure 2-43.

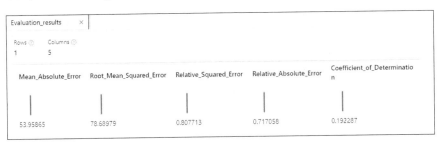

FIGURE 2-43 Metrics for a regression model

As you can see from these metrics, this model does not perform well with high error values and a low coefficient of determination. We will need to select additional features and train the model to see if we can create a better performing model.

Figure 2-44 shows the metrics for a classification model using our student dataset and using the hours studied and completed labs as features and pass as the label.

As you can see from these metrics, with a threshold set to 50%, the model is only 50% accurate with a precision of 33%. We will need to add additional data, use a different algorithm or perform feature engineering, and train the model to see if we can create a better performing model.

Earlier in the chapter, we discussed bias in the dataset, where the algorithm is unable to separate the true signal from the noise. This is often caused by the dataset used for training. If we have used a split of the same dataset for scoring and evaluating, then the model may appear to perform well but does not generalize—in other words, it does not predict well with new unseen data.

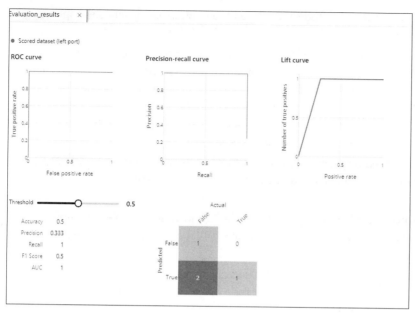

FIGURE 2-44 Metrics for a classification model

This is one of the most common problems with machine learning and is known as overfitting. *Overfitting* means that the model does not generalize well from training data to unseen data, especially data that is unlike the training data. Common causes are bias in the training data or too many features selected, meaning the model cannot distinguish between the signal and the noise.

One way to avoid overfitting is to perform cross validation. In *cross validation*, a dataset is repeatedly split into a training dataset and a validation dataset. Each split is used to train and test the model. Cross-validation evaluates both the dataset and the model, and it provides an idea of how representative the dataset is and how sensitive the model is to variations in input data.

Describe model deployment and management

Azure Machine Learning allows you to create and manage versions of your model and then choose which version of a model to deploy so that applications can use the model to make predictions.

In machine learning, *inferencing* refers to the use of a trained model to make predictions for new unseen data. A machine learning model can be used for:

- **Real-time** For individual or small numbers of data observations.
- **Batch** For large volumes of data.

For batch inference processing, you create a pipeline that includes steps to load the input data, load the model, predict labels, and write the results to a datastore, normally to a file or to a database.

For real-time processing, the model is deployed as a web service that enables applications to request via http.

If you have used a pipeline to build your model, you can create an inference pipeline that performs the same steps for new data input, not the sample data used in training. You can publish the inference pipeline as a web service. A real-time inference pipeline must have at least one Web Service Input module and one Web Service Output module. The Web Service Input module is normally the first step in the pipeline. The pipeline performs the same steps for new data input. The Web Service Output module is normally the final step in the pipeline.

In Azure Machine Learning, when you publish a real-time inferencing model, you deploy the model as a web service running in a Docker container. There are three ways you can deploy the container:

- **Azure Kubernetes Service (AKS) cluster**   AKS is Microsoft's implementation of Kubernetes and is used to run highly scalable real-time interference as a web service for production.
- **Azure Container Instance (ACI)**   ACI is used to run a single Docker container. You can use this to expose your prediction model as a web service for testing and low-volume production scenarios.
- **IoT Edge**   Azure IoT Edge supports the running of containers containing machine learning models on small devices, reducing the need for network traffic and reducing latency.

You can also use ONNX (Open Neural Network Exchange) to export your model and deploy it on other platforms, such as on a mobile device.

Skill 2.4: Describe capabilities of no-code machine learning with Azure Machine Learning

Azure Machine Learning has two tools for building machine learning models with low or no code. This section describes how you use these Azure Machine Learning tools to build and deploy machine learning models.

> **This skill covers how to:**
> - Describe Azure Automated Machine Learning
> - Describe Azure Machine Learning designer

Describe Azure Automated Machine Learning

Azure Automated Machine Learning (AutoML) finds the best algorithm for the dataset. A number of iterations are run to evaluate different algorithms and features. The results are analyzed and ranked, and an explanation is produced that interprets the best model for the data, parameters, and task.

Figure 2-45 shows the Automated ML process, where data is fed into Automated ML, which then outputs a best-fit trained model.

FIGURE 2-45 Automated ML

Automated ML trades data science skills with compute power and time. A data scientist will evaluate and choose the features, algorithm, and hyperparameters for the model. Automated ML simply tries all combinations of algorithm, features, and parameters and then ranks the results by the chosen metric.

Clicking on Automated ML in the left-hand navigation pane in the Azure Machine Learning studio lists all previous ML runs and allows you to create a new run. Clicking on + New Automated ML run opens the Create a new Automated ML run pane, as shown in Figure 2-46.

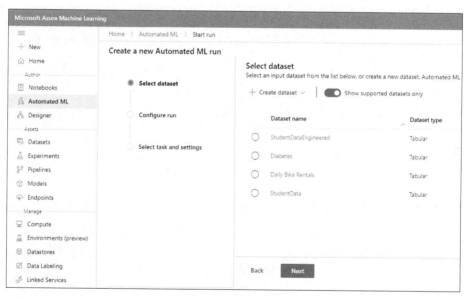

FIGURE 2-46 Create a new Automated ML run – select dataset

The first step when creating an Automated ML run is to select a dataset. The datasets added to the workspace are listed, and you can register a new dataset at this stage if required. Selecting a dataset and clicking Next displays the next step in the wizard, as shown in Figure 2-47.

The second step when creating an Automated ML run is to give the experiment a name, to select the compute for training, but most importantly to select the label.

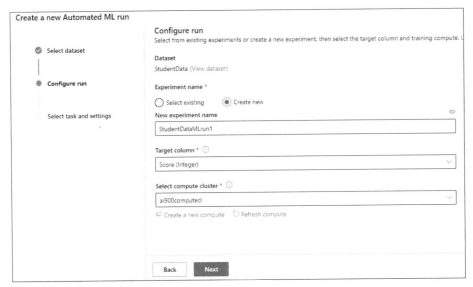

FIGURE 2-47 Create a new Automated ML run – configure run

 EXAM TIP

Automated ML only supports supervised learning, as you must specify a label for the model to fit the data to.

Clicking Next displays the final step in the wizard, as shown in Figure 2-48.

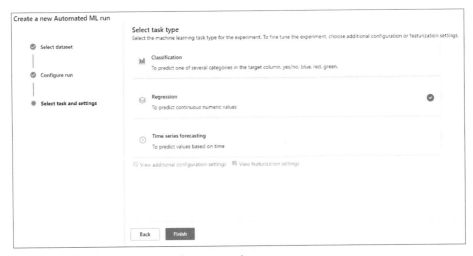

FIGURE 2-48 Create a new Automated ML run – task type

The second step when creating an Automated ML run is to select the model type. You can choose from classification, regression, and time-series forecasting.

Clicking View additional configuration settings enables you to select the metric used to evaluate the best model and to change how long the run will last, as shown in Figure 2-49.

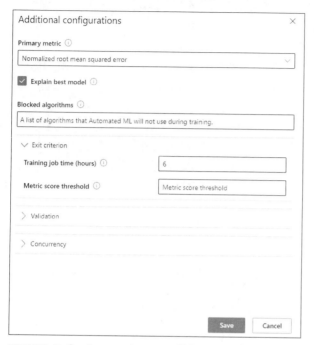

FIGURE 2-49 Create a new Automated ML run – additional configuration

In additional configurations, you can select the metric used to evaluate and rank the models that are generated by Automated ML. By default, Automated ML will evaluate all algorithms available, and you can exclude specific algorithms if required. Automated ML will run for six hours by default. You can change the number of hours for Automated ML, and you can set the threshold for the selected metric; when this threshold value is met, the training job will terminate.

Figure 2-50 shows the results of the run.

This summary page for the Automated ML run shows the status of the run and the best model. Clicking on the Models tab allows you to review each of the models and evaluate the metrics, as shown in Figure 2-51.

In Chapter 1, we discussed the principle of Transparency and how you sometimes need to be able to explain how an AI algorithm has generated its results. Automated ML generates an explanation for the model that was identified as the best model. The explanation allows you to understand why the model was selected and how the model works. It enables you to meet regulatory requirements and provides transparency to users.

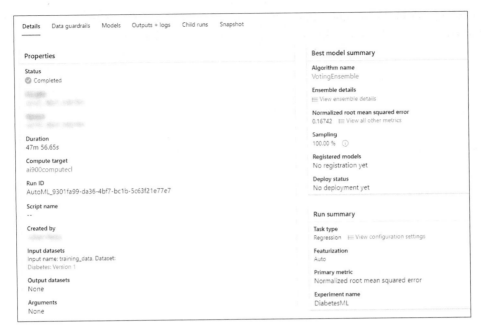

FIGURE 2-50 Automated ML run details

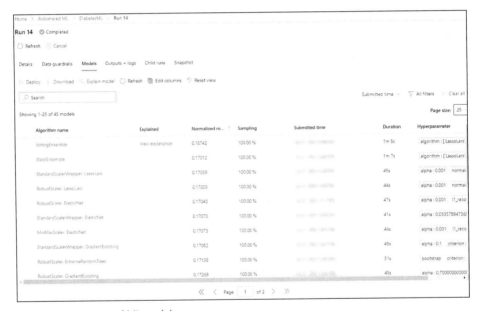

FIGURE 2-51 Automated ML models

Clicking on View explanation shows several different insights into the best model—for example, the most influential features, as shown in Figure 2-52.

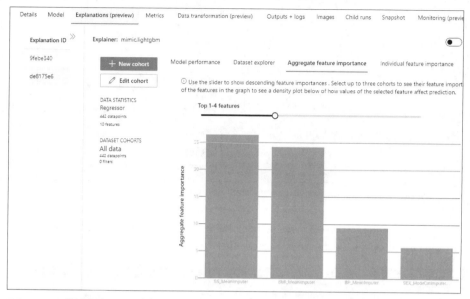

FIGURE 2-52 Explain best model

You can use the information shown in the explanations to interpret the model and build responsible models.

You can select the model and deploy it from within Automated ML to either Azure Container Instances or to Azure Kubernetes Service. This will register the model and deploy it as a web service.

Describe Azure Machine Learning designer

Azure Machine Learning designer is a visual drag-and-drop tool for creating machine learning pipelines. Azure Machine Learning designer simplifies the process of building, testing, and deploying models.

Azure Machine Learning designer contains modules for data preparation, training, data visualization, and model evaluation.

Designer overview

Clicking on Designer in the left-hand navigation pane in the Azure Machine Learning studio lists existing pipelines and allows you to create a new pipeline, either from a blank pipeline or by using sample templates, as shown in Figure 2-53.

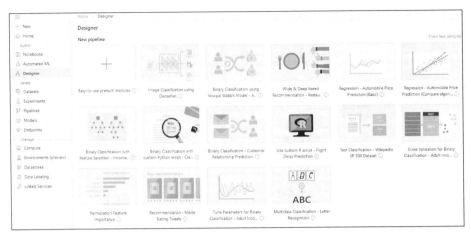

FIGURE 2-53 Azure Machine Learning designer

Selecting the second sample—Binary Classification using Vowpal Wabbit Model - Adult Income Prediction—opens the designer, as shown in Figure 2-54.

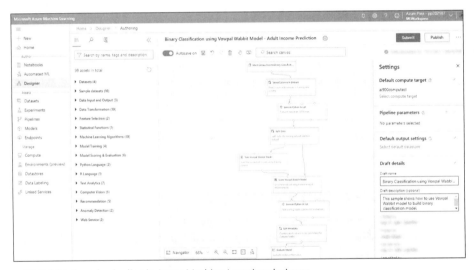

FIGURE 2-54 Sample pipeline in Azure Machine Learning designer

In the left pane of the designer, you see the datasets in the workspace and all modules that you can add to the designer canvas. In the middle pane of the designer, you can see the workflow for the pipeline, with a dataset as the first step at the top and the final evaluate step at the bottom. In the right-hand pane, you can see the settings for the pipeline, including the compute cluster selected.

Although you can use the designer as a no-code tool, you can also insert steps into the workflow to run Python and R scripts.

Clicking on Submit will run the pipeline. As the pipeline is running, the currently active step is highlighted, so you follow the progress of the pipeline run, as shown in Figure 2-55.

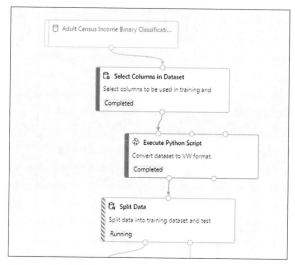

FIGURE 2-55 Pipeline in progress

You can click on a step and see its properties. For example, the Split Data step properties show the mode for splitting the data and the proportion to split, as shown in Figure 2-56.

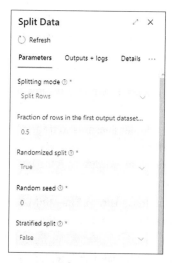

FIGURE 2-56 Step properties

When the pipeline run has completed, you can view the metrics generated for the model by right-clicking on the Evaluate Model step, as shown in Figure 2-57.

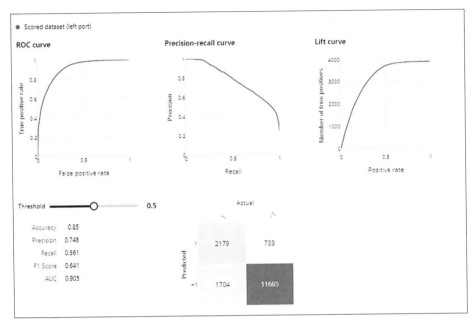

FIGURE 2-57 Evaluation metrics

Create a new model with the designer

If you want to create a new model, you start by creating a blank training pipeline that ingests and preprocesses a dataset, and then trains and evaluates the model, as shown in Figure 2-58.

Datasets has been expanded in the left-hand pane, showing four datasets that include the student exam results dataset we registered earlier in this chapter. Training pipelines always starts with a dataset. You can drag your chosen dataset and drop it onto the canvas, as shown in Figure 2-59.

Before training, data often must be cleansed. There are many modules available to transform and cleanse data. If you have numeric features, you should normalize them. You need to drag the Normalize Data tile onto the canvas. Next, you need to drag the output from the bottom of the dataset step to the top of the normalize step, as shown in Figure 2-60.

In the Normalize Data properties, you should select the method to transform. The MinMax method scales all values to a range between 0 and 1. You need to select the numeric columns to normalize.

Next, a Split Data module is used to randomly split the dataset into training and validation subsets. This is a common step in a supervised learning pipeline so that you can evaluate the model using data not used for training. You can specify the ratio of data used for training and for testing.

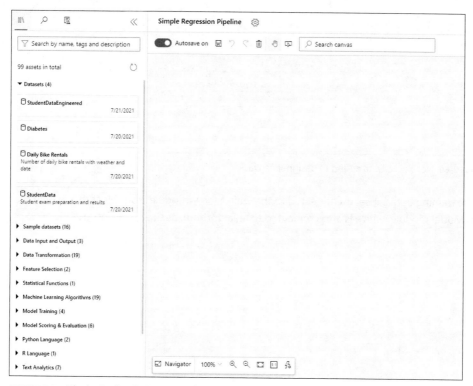

FIGURE 2-58 Blank pipeline in Azure Machine Learning designer

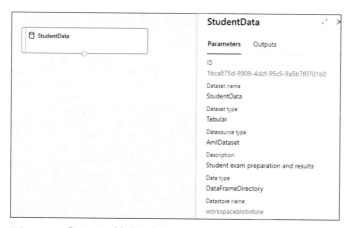

FIGURE 2-59 Dataset added to designer canvas

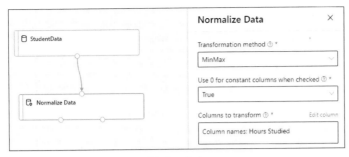

FIGURE 2-60 Normalize Data added to designer canvas

The training data subset is connected to the Train Model module. You select the label in the Train Model module, which is also connected to an algorithm, as shown in Figure 2-61.

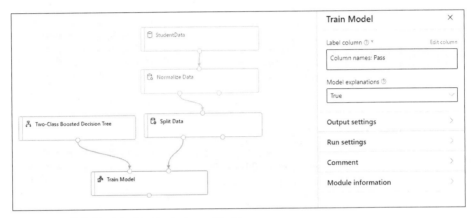

FIGURE 2-61 Train Model added to designer canvas

After training, a Score Model module is used to score the testing dataset from the Split Data step, as shown in Figure 2-62.

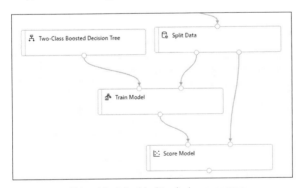

FIGURE 2-62 Score Model added to designer canvas

The Score Model module is required before you can evaluate the model. The Score Model module is added between the Train Model and Evaluate Model steps in the pipeline. Score Model has two inputs, one from the Train Model and the other from Split Data. You take the second output from the Split Data step and connect to the second input on the Score Model.

The testing data includes the actual label values. We can compare the actual values to the predicted labels generated in the Score Model step and use the Evaluate Model module to calculate the metrics to help us determine the performance, or accuracy, of the model. The complete pipeline is shown in Figure 2-63.

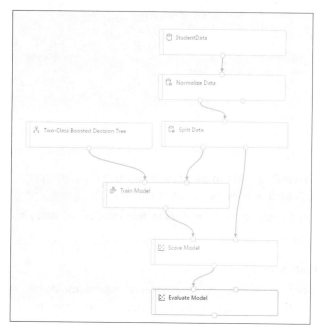

FIGURE 2-63 Evaluate Model added to designer canvas

This pipeline is the common workflow to train a supervised model, such as regression or classification. You may add steps between the dataset and normalize data to select columns, cleanse data, and transform data depending on your dataset and requirements.

Clicking on Submit will open a new window to start a run of the pipeline, as shown in Figure 2-64.

FIGURE 2-64 Set up pipeline run

To run a pipeline, an experiment is required. You can either use an existing experiment or create a new experiment. Clicking on Submit queues the pipeline to be run.

Once the pipeline run has completed, you can use the metrics to determine the accuracy of the model.

Deploy a model with the designer

Once you are content with the model's performance, you can register the model. You do this by accessing the Outputs + logs tab in the properties on the Train Model step, as shown in Figure 2-65.

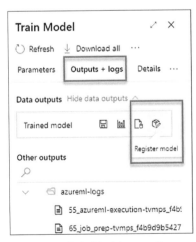

FIGURE 2-65 Train Model properties

Clicking on the Register model button displays a dialog with the name of the model. You can see the models in the Machine Learning studio, as shown in Figure 2-66.

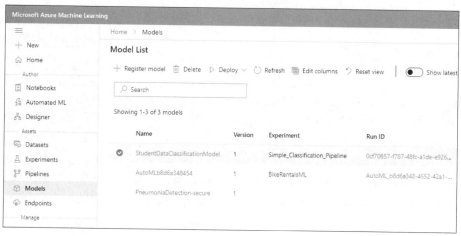

FIGURE 2-66 Model list

To use the model, you can either clone the pipeline and add in steps for batch processing or create a real-time inference pipeline. For a real-time inference pipeline, you need to replace the dataset with a Web Service Input module, remove the evaluate steps, and replace with a Web Service Output module, as shown in Figure 2-67.

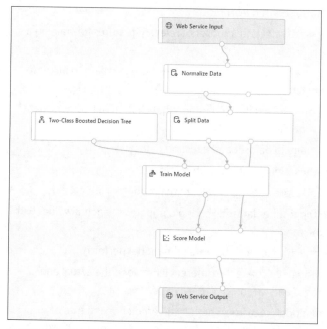

FIGURE 2-67 Web Service Input and Output in a real-time inference pipeline

You can select the model and deploy it from within Azure Machine Learning studio to either Azure Container Instances or to Azure Kubernetes Service. This deploys the model as a web service.

Chapter summary

In this chapter, you learned some of the general concepts related to Artificial Intelligence. You learned about the feature of common AI workloads, and you learned about the principles of responsible AI. Here are the key concepts from this chapter:

- Machine learning is the basis for modern AI.
- Machine learning uses data to train models.
- Feature is the name for the data used as inputs to a model.
- Label is the name for the data that the model predicts.
- Supervised learning requires data with features and labels to train the model.
- Unsupervised learning trains with data without labels.
- Regression models predict a value along a range of values.
- Classification models predict a discrete class or category.
- Regression and classification models are both examples of supervised learning.
- Clustering models group data by similarities in the data into discrete categories.
- Clustering is an example of unsupervised learning.
- Feature selection is the process of selecting a subset of relevant features for training a machine learning model.
- Feature engineering is the process of creating new features from raw data to increase the predictive power of the machine learning model.
- Normalization is a common process in data preparation that changes all numeric data to use the same scale to prevent bias.
- You split your dataset into a training dataset and a testing dataset.
- Training a model combines the training dataset with an algorithm.
- After training is complete, you score and then evaluate the model.
- Scoring is performed using the testing dataset. Scoring compares the actual values with the predicted values from the model.
- Evaluation generates metrics that determine how well the model performs.
- The metrics for regression models calculate the difference between the actual and predicted values using averages and means.
- The metrics for classification models measure whether the prediction is a true or false positive or negative. A confusion matrix represents the number of true/false positive/negative predictions. The metrics for classification models are ratios of these predictions.

- You need an Azure subscription to use Machine Learning on Azure.
- You need to create an Azure Machine Learning workspace to build and train models.
- The Azure Machine Learning workspace manages assets associated with machine learning, including datastores, datasets, experiments, models, and compute.
- Compute instances support data preparation and building of models.
- Compute clusters support training of models.
- You can deploy a model to Azure Container Instances or Azure Kubernetes Service.
- Azure Machine Learning studio can be used to author models using Python with Jupyter notebooks, using Automated ML, or using the drag-and-drop designer.
- .NET is not supported in Azure Machine Learning studio.
- You can build and manage models using Visual Studio Code with .NET and Python.
- Automated ML uses the power of the cloud to create multiple models for the same data using different algorithms and then determining which is the best fit model.
- Azure Machine Learning designer is a graphical user interface that allows you to drag and drop modules into a workflow to build a model.

Thought experiment

In this thought experiment, demonstrate your skills and knowledge of the topics covered in this chapter. You can find the answers in the section that follows.

You work for Relecloud, an internet service provider that collects large volumes of data about its customers and the services they use.

You are evaluating the potential use of machine learning models to improve business decision making and in business operations.

Relecloud uses Azure for virtual machines but has no experience of machine learning in Azure.

You need to advise on the types of machine learning models to build and the languages and tools that you should use within your organization.

You also need to explain to IT what Azure resources are required to be provisioned to use machine learning in Relecloud's applications.

Answer the following questions:

1. Which machine learning type should you use to determine if a social media post has positive or negative sentiment?
2. Which type of machine learning groups unlabeled data using similarities in the data?
3. Which two datasets do you split your data into when building a machine learning model?
4. Which metrics can you use to evaluate a regression machine learning model?
5. Which metrics can you use to evaluate a classification machine learning model?

6. Which compute target should you use for development of machine learning models?

7. What is used to increase the predictive power of a machine learning model?

8. What should you do to prevent your model from being biased by one feature?

9. What should you do to enable a trained machine learning model to be measured for accuracy?

10. What should you do after training your model prior to deploying your model as a web service?

11. You use Automated ML to find the best model for your data. Which option should you use to interpret and provide transparency for the model selected?

12. Which two types of datasets can you register and use to train Automatic Machine Learning (AutoML) models?

Thought experiment answers

This section contains the solutions to the thought experiment. Each answer explains why the answer choice is correct.

1. The classification machine learning model is used to predict mutually exclusive categories. Classification involves learning using labels to classify data. Two-class classification algorithms can provide an either/or answer such as a social media post having a positive or negative sentiment.

2. The clustering machine learning model analyzes unlabeled data to find similarities in data points and groups them together into clusters. The clustering algorithm segments data into multiple groups based on similarities in the data.

3. The dataset is split into a training dataset and a testing dataset. The testing dataset is often referred to as the validation dataset.

4. Root mean squared error (RMSE) is used to evaluate regression models. RMSE is a measure of the difference between predictions and actual values. The closer RMSE is to 0, the better the model is performing. You can also use Coefficient of Determination.

5. Precision is a measure of the correct positive results. Precision is the number of true positives divided by the sum of the number of true positives and false positives. Precision is scored between 0 and 1, with closer to 1 being better. You can also use Accuracy and F-Score.

6. A compute instance is a configured development environment for machine learning.

7. Feature engineering is the process of creating new features from raw data to increase the predictive power of the machine learning model.

8. Normalization is the method that adjusts the values in numeric columns so that all numeric values are on a common scale, normally between 0 and 1. A dataset that has values using different scales can bias the model toward that feature.

9. You should score the model. After a model has been trained, the model should be evaluated using a different set of data. Scoring applies the validation dataset to the trained model to generate predictions that can be evaluated using metrics that measure the accuracy of the predictions.

10. After training your model, you need to create an inference pipeline that performs the same steps for new data input, not the sample data used in training.

11. Explain best model generates an explanation for the model that was identified as the best model.

12. File and tabular datasets can be used in Azure Machine Learning training workflows.

Describe features of computer vision workloads on Azure

Cognitive Services is a suite of prebuilt AI services that developers can use to build AI solutions. Cognitive Services meet common AI requirements that allow you to add AI to your apps more quickly with less expertise.

This chapter explains the pre-built AI provided in Azure: Cognitive Services. The chapter will begin with an overview of all Cognitive Services but then will focus on one of the major components of Cognitive Services, the Computer Vision service.

Computer vision is the processing of still images and video streams. Computer vision can interpret the image and provide detail and understanding about the image in computer readable form.

The concepts involved in computer vision will be outlined with use cases, followed by how to use the Azure Cognitive Services Computer Vision service.

This chapter provides an overview of Cognitive Services and the details of the Computer Vision service. Chapter 4 will explain the other major component of Cognitive Services, Natural Language Processing.

Skills covered in this chapter:

- Skill 3.1: Identify common types of computer vision solution
- Skill 3.2: Identify Azure tools and services for computer vision tasks

Skill 3.1: Identify common types of computer vision solution

Computer vision is the processing of still images and video streams and extracting information from those images. Computer vision can interpret the image and provide detail and understanding about the image in a computer-readable form. Computers can take this information and perform further processing and analysis. Many applications use computer vision to enhance user experience or to capture information about objects and people.

Microsoft Azure provides a set of services around computer vision as part of Azure Cognitive Services. You can also use Azure Machine Learning to create your own image-processing models.

A focus of the Microsoft Azure AI Fundamentals certification is on the capabilities and features of computer vision and how computer vision can be applied in solutions. This requires you to understand the use cases for computer vision and to be able to differentiate the various services for computer vision in Microsoft Azure.

This skill covers how to:

- Introduce Cognitive Services
- Understand computer vision
- Describe image classification
- Describe object detection
- Describe optical character recognition
- Describe facial detection, recognition, and analysis

Introduce Cognitive Services

Before we look at computer vision, we need to describe Cognitive Services and how you configure Cognitive Services for use.

Cognitive Services are prebuilt machine learning models trained by Microsoft with massive volumes of data that developers can use to build AI solutions without requiring ML skills. Cognitive Services are focused on a subset of common AI requirements around processing images and analyzing text.

Cognitive Services are available as a set of REST APIs that can easily be deployed and consumed by applications. Essentially, Cognitive Services are off-the-shelf services that help you develop an AI-based solution more quickly and with less specialist expertise.

Overview of Cognitive Services

Cognitive Services are a family of AI services and APIs that you can use to build intelligent solutions. Cognitive Services enable applications to see, hear, speak, search, understand, and begin with decision-making.

This family of AI services is categorized into five groups:

- Decision
- Language
- Speech
- Vision
- Web search

The group of services in the Decision group helps you make smarter decisions:

- **Anomaly Detector**   Quickly identify potential problems by detecting unusual data points or trends in time-series data.
- **Metrics Advisor**   Built on Anomaly Detector, this service identifies the key areas for root cause analysis. Metrics Advisor helps focus on fixing issues rather than monitoring.
- **Content Moderator**   Detect potentially offensive or undesirable text, image, and video content. Content Moderator provides a review tool, where a human can validate flagged content and improve the sensitivity of moderation.
- **Personalizer**   Creates a personalized experience for a user based on his/her behavior. This could be content shown on a website or providing a different layout. Personalizer is an example of reinforcement learning.

The group of services in the Language group extract meaning from unstructured text:

- **Immersive Reader**   Helps readers of all ages and abilities to comprehend text using audio and visual cues. Immersive Reader can be used to improve literacy.
- **Language Understanding**   Builds natural language understanding into apps, bots, and IoT devices. Language Understanding interprets the intent and extracts key information from supplied text.
- **QnA Maker**   Creates a conversational question and answer layer on your existing FAQ and company information. QnA Maker is explained in Chapter 5.
- **Text Analytics**   Discovers insights from textual data. Text Analytics is one of the most used Cognitive Services. You can detect the sentiment of sentences or whole paragraphs. You can extract key phrases from a piece of text, and extract entities such as people, places, and things from a piece of text. Text Analytics supports a wide range of languages.
- **Translator**   Detects and translates text in real-time or in batch across more than 90 languages.

The Language services are the focus of Chapter 4.

The group of services in the Speech group allows you to add speech processing into your apps:

- **Speech to Text**   Transcribes audio into readable, searchable text in real-time or from audio files.
- **Text to Speech**   Synthesizes text into lifelike speech.
- **Speech Translation**   Converts audio into text and translates into another language in real-time. Speech Translation utilizes the Translator services.
- **Speaker Recognition**   Identifies people from the voices in an audio clip.

The Speech services are covered in Chapter 4.

The group of services in the Vision group helps you extract information from images and videos:

- **Computer Vision service** Analyzes content in images and video and extracts details from the images.
- **Custom Vision** Trains computer vision with your own set of images that meets your business requirements.
- **Face** Detects faces in images and describes their features and emotions. Face can also recognize and verify people from images.
- **Form Recognizer** Extracts text, key-value pairs, and tables from documents.
- **Video Analyzer for Media** Analyzes the visual and audio channels of a video and indexes its content.

The rest of this chapter will focus on these Vision services.

The group of services in the Web Search group allows you to utilize the Bing search engine to search millions of webpages for images, news, product, and company information. These services have been moved from Cognitive Services to a separate service, Bing Web Search.

As you can see, Cognitive Services consist of a broad, and growing, set of AI services. A common feature of these services is that they require no training and can easily be consumed by applications with a REST API call.

We will now look at how you can deploy Cognitive Services in Azure.

Deploy Cognitive Services

Cognitive Services are easily deployed in Azure as resources. You can use the Azure portal, the CLI, or PowerShell to create resources for Cognitive Services. There are even ARM templates available to simplify deployment further.

Once created, the APIs in Cognitive Services will then be available to developers through REST APIs and client library SDKs.

You have two options when creating resources for Cognitive:

- Multi-service resource
- Single-service resource

With a multi-service resource, you have access to all the Cognitive Services with a single key and https endpoint. Benefits of a multi-service resource are the following:

- Only one resource to create and manage
- Access to Vision, Language, Search, and Speech services using a single API
- Consolidates billing across all services

With a single-service resource, you access a single Cognitive Service with a unique key and https endpoint for each individual service. Benefits of a single-service resource are the following:

- Limits the services that a developer can use
- Dedicated API for each service
- Separate billing of services
- Free tier available

The multi-service resource is named Cognitive Services in the Azure portal. To create a multi-service Cognitive Services resource in the Azure portal, search for Cognitive Services and pick Cognitive Services by Microsoft.

Figure 3-1 shows the service description for the Cognitive Services multi-resource service.

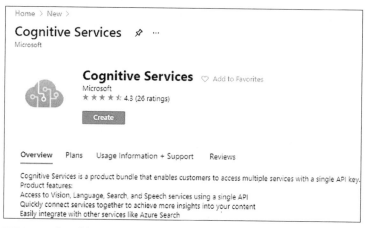

FIGURE 3-1 Cognitive Services multi-resource service description

After clicking on the Create button, the Create Cognitive Services pane opens, as shown in Figure 3-2.

You will need to select the subscription, resource group, and region where the resource is to be deployed. You will then need to create a unique name for the service. This name will be the domain name for your endpoint and so must be unique worldwide. You should then select your pricing tier. There is only one pricing tier for the multi-service resource, Standard S0.

Clicking on Review + create will validate the options. You then click on Create to create the resource. The resource will be deployed in a few seconds.

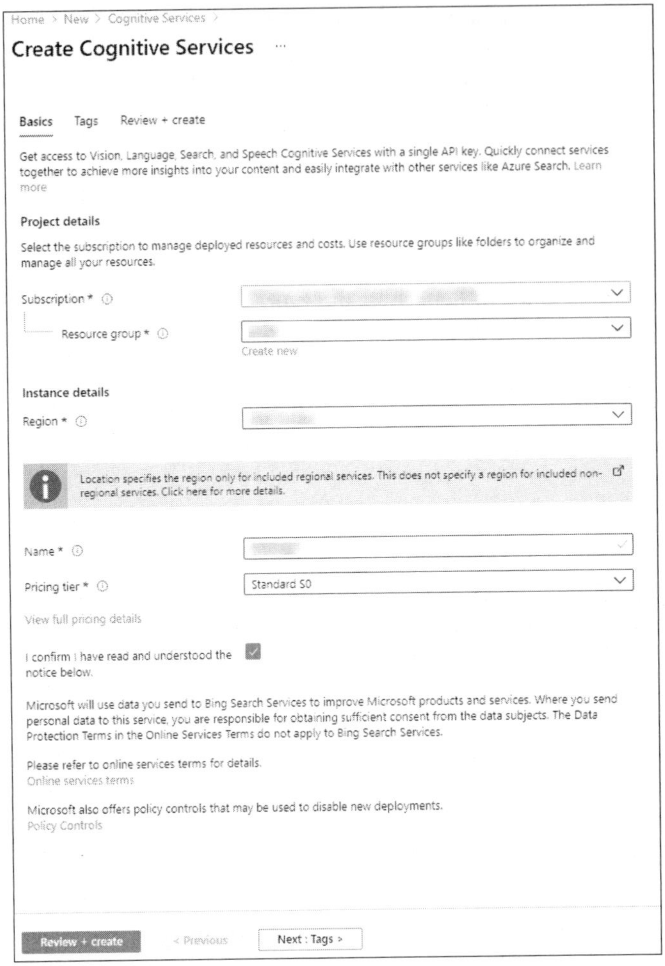

FIGURE 3-2 Creating a Cognitive Services resource

You can create a Cognitive Services resource using the CLI as follows:

```
az cognitiveservices account create --name <unique name> --resource-group <resource
group name> --kind CognitiveServices --sku S0 --location <region> --yes
```

To create a single-service resource for the Computer Vision service using the Azure portal, you should search for Computer Vision and create the resource. The options are the same as the multi-service resource, except you can select the Free pricing tier.

You can create a Computer Vision resource using the CLI as follows:

```
az cognitiveservices account create --name <unique name> --resource-group <resource
group name> --kind ComputerVision --sku F0 --location <region> --yes
```

If you want to create other single-service resources, use the following CLI command to find the correct values for kind:

```
az cognitiveservices account list-kinds
```

Once your resource has been created, you will need to obtain the REST API URL and the key to access the resource.

Use Cognitive Services securely

Once created, each resource will have a unique endpoint for the REST API and authentication keys. You will need these details to use Cognitive Services from your app.

To view the endpoint and keys in the Azure portal, navigate to the resource and click on Keys and Endpoint, as shown in Figure 3-3.

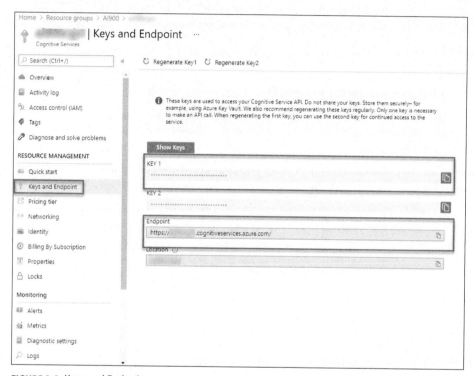

FIGURE 3-3 Keys and Endpoint

You can access the keys using the CLI as follows:

```
az cognitiveservices account keys list --name <unique name> --resource-group <resource group name>
```

EXAM TIP

Practice creating single- and multi-service resources in the Azure portal and make sure you know where the endpoint and keys can be found.

Containers for Cognitive Services

Cognitive Services are also available as Docker containers for deployment to IoT devices and to on-premises systems. Containers provide advantages with hybrid and disconnected scenarios and allow higher throughput with lower latency of data.

Only some Cognitive Services are available in containers.

NEED MORE REVIEW? **AZURE COGNITIVE SERVICES CONTAINERS**

For more information on using Cognitive Services with containers AI, see https://docs.microsoft.com/azure/cognitive-services/cognitive-services-container-support.

Understand computer vision

Computer vision is the interaction with the world through visual perception. Computer vision processes still images and video streams to interpret the images, providing details and understanding about the images.

A computer sees an array holding the color and intensity as number values. Computer vision analyzes these values using pre-built models to detect and interpret the image.

Computer vision makes it easy for developers to process and label visual content in their apps. The Computer Vision service API can describe objects in images, detect the existence of people, and generate human-readable descriptions and tags, enabling developers to categorize and process visual content.

Key features of computer vision

Some other key features of computer vision include the ability to:

- Categorize images
- Determine the image width and height
- Detect common objects including people
- Analyze faces
- Detect adult content

Use cases for computer vision

There are many uses for computer vision:

- In retail stores, a network of cameras can detect a shopper taking an object from the shelf and adding it to their basket.
- In vehicles, cameras can be used to detect pedestrians and cyclists, warning the driver of vulnerable road users.
- In healthcare, computer vision can analyze images of skin conditions to determine the severity with much higher accuracy than human specialists.

- In utilities, the positions of the panels on solar farms can be analyzed using cameras mounted on drones and the orientation changed to maximize efficiency.

Describe image classification

Image classification is a machine learning model that predicts the category, or class, the contents of the image belong to. A set of images is used to train the model. A new image can then be categorized using the model.

There are 86 standard categories that can be detected in an image. Categories are different to tags. Tags are based on the objects, people, and actions identified in the image.

Image classification can:

- Describe an image
- Categorize an image
- Tag an image

Figure 3-4 shows an example of image classification with a textual description of the image added to the bottom of the image.

A cat sitting on a counter

FIGURE 3-4 Example of image classification

Detecting the color scheme in an image is an example of image classification. Colors are classified in the image: the dominant foreground color, the dominant background color, and the accent color, which is the most vibrant color in the image.

Identifying products on a warehouse shelf is an example of image classification. The model will check for products against trained images added to the model.

Quality control on a manufacturing line is another example of image classification. Product labels and bottle caps can be verified to be correctly attached using image classification against a set of trained images of correctly labeled and sealed products.

Describe object detection

Object detection identifies and tags individual visual features (objects) in an image. Object detection can recognize many different types of objects.

Object detection will also return the coordinates for a box surrounding a tagged visual feature. Object detection is like image classification, but object detection also returns the location of each tagged object in an image.

Object detection can:

- Detect common objects
- Tag visual features
- Detect faces
- Identify brands and products
- Identify landmarks

Figure 3-5 shows an example of object detection. Three cats have been identified as objects and their coordinates indicated by the boxes drawn on the image.

FIGURE 3-5 Example of object detection

Object detection can be used to detect objects in an image. For example, you could train computer vision to detect people wearing face masks. Facial detection does not include the ability to recognize that a face is covered with a mask, and masks may prevent faces from being recognized.

Evaluating compliance with building safety regulations is another example of object detection. Images of a building interior and exterior can be used to identify fire extinguishers, doors, and other access and emergency exits.

Describe optical character recognition

Optical character recognition (OCR) extracts small amounts of text from an image. OCR can recognize individual shapes as letters, numerals, punctuation, and other elements of text.

OCR can:

- Extract printed text
- Extract handwritten text

Using OCR, you can extract details from invoices that have been sent electronically or scanned from paper. These details can then be validated against the expected details in your finance system.

Figure 3-6 shows an example of using OCR to extract text from an image.

FIGURE 3-6 Example of image classification

The OCR service extracted the following pieces of text from the image:

- 220-240V ~AC
- hp
- LaserJet Pro M102w
- Europe - Multilingual localization
- Serial No.
- VNF 4C29992

- Product No.
- G3Q35A
- Option B19
- Regulatory Model Number
- SHNGC-1500-01
- Made in Vietnam

Describe facial detection, recognition, and analysis

Facial detection can provide a series of attributes about a face it has detected, including whether the person is wearing eyeglasses or has a beard. Facial detection can also estimate the type of eye covering, including sunglasses and swimming goggles.

Facial detection and recognition can:

- Detect faces
- Analyze facial features
- Recognize faces
- Identify famous people

Object detection includes the detection of faces in an image but only provides basic attributes of the face, including age and gender. Facial detection goes much further in analyzing many other facial characteristics, such as emotion.

Figure 3-7 shows an example of facial detection of the author.

FIGURE 3-7 Example of facial detection

The facial detection identified the face, drew a box around the face, and supplied details such as wearing glasses, neutral emotion, not smiling, and other facial characteristics.

Customer engagement in retail is an example of using facial recognition to identify customers when they walk into a retail store.

Validating identity for access to business premises is an example of facial detection and recognition. Facial detection and recognition can identify a person in an image, and this can be used to permit access to a secure location.

Recognition of famous people is a feature of domain-specific content where thousands of well-known peoples' images have been added to the computer vision model. Images can be tagged with the names of celebrities.

Face detection can be used to monitor a driver's face. The angle, or head poise, can be determined, and this can be used to tell if the driver is looking at the road ahead, looking down at a mobile device, or showing signs of tiredness.

Now that you have learned about the concepts of computer vision, let's look at the specific Computer Vision services provided by Azure Cognitive Services.

Skill 3.2: Identify Azure tools and services for computer vision tasks

Azure Cognitive Services provide pre-trained computer vision models that cover most of the capabilities required for analyzing images and videos.

This section describes the capabilities of the computer vision services in Azure Cognitive Services.

A focus of the Microsoft Azure AI Fundamentals certification is on the capabilities of the Computer Vision service. This requires you to understand how to use the Computer Vision service and especially how to create your own custom models with the Custom Vision service.

EXAM TIP

You will need to be able to distinguish between the Computer Vision, Custom Vision, and Face services.

This skill covers how to:
- Understand the capabilities of the Computer Vision service
- Understand the Custom Vision service
- Understand the Face service
- Understand the Form Recognizer service

Understand the capabilities of the Computer Vision service

The Computer Vision service in Azure Cognitive Services provides a few different algorithms to analyze images. For instance, Computer Vision can do the following:
- Detect and locate over 10,000 classes of common objects.
- Detect and analyze human faces.
- Generate a single sentence description of an image.

- Generate a set of tags that relate to the contents of the image.
- Identify images that contain adult, racy, or gory content.
- Detect and extract the text from an image.

To use Computer Vision, you will need to create a Cognitive Services multi-service resource, or a Computer Vision single-service resource, as described earlier in this chapter.

The following sections describe the capabilities of the APIs in the Computer Vision service.

Analyze image

The analyze operation extracts visual features from the image content.

The image can either be uploaded or, more commonly, you specify a URL to where the image is stored.

You specify the features that you want to extract. If you do not specify any features, the image categories are returned.

The request URL is formulated as follows:

```
https://{endpoint}/vision/v3.1/analyze[?visualFeatures][&details][&language]
```

The URL for the image is contained in the body of the request.

The visual features that you can request are the following:

- **Adult**   Detects if the image is pornographic (adult), contains sexually suggestive content (racy), or depicts violence or blood (gory).
- **Brands**   Detects well-known brands within an image.
- **Categories**   Categorizes image content according to a taxonomy of 86 categories.
- **Color**   Determines the accent color, dominant color, and whether an image is black and white.
- **Description**   Describes the image content with a complete sentence.
- **Faces**   Detects if there are human faces in the image with their coordinates, gender, and age.
- **ImageType**   Detects if the image is clipart or a line drawing.
- **Objects**   Detects various objects within an image, including their coordinates.
- **Tags**   Tags the image with a detailed list of words related to the content.

The details parameter is used to extract domain-specific details:

- **Celebrities**   Identifies celebrities in the image.
- **Landmarks**   Identifies landmarks in the image.

The language parameter supports a few languages. The default is en, English. Currently, English is the only supported language for tagging and categorizing images.

The Computer Vision service only supports file sizes less than 4MB. Images must be greater than 50x50 pixels and be in either of the JPEG, PNG, GIF, or BMP formats.

Below is the JSON returned for the image of the three cats used earlier in this chapter for these categories: adult, color, and imageType features.

```
"categories": [{

"name": "animal_cat",    "score": 0.79296875  }],

 "adult": {   "isAdultContent": false,   "isRacyContent": false,   "isGoryContent":
false,   "adultScore": 0.010710394941270351,   "racyScore": 0.01310222502797842,
"goreScore": 0.05890617147088051  },

 "color": {   "dominantColorForeground": "Black",   "dominantColorBackground": "Grey",
"dominantColors": ["Black", "Grey", "White"],   "accentColor": "635D4F",   "isBWImg":
false },

 "imageType": {   "clipArtType": 0,   "lineDrawingType": 0  },
```

The category has been correctly identified with a confidence of 79.2%. There is no adult content in the image. The main colors are black, white, and grey.

The analyze operation provides a generic image analysis returning many different visual features. There are other operations that extract other information from the image or provide more detail than that provided by the analyze operation.

Describe image

The describe operation generates description(s) of an image using complete sentences. Content tags are generated from the various objects in the image.

One or more descriptions are generated. The sentences are evaluated, and confidence scores are generated. A list of captions is returned ordered from the highest confidence score to the lowest.

The request URL is formulated as follows:

```
https://{endpoint}/vision/v3.1/describe[?maxCandidates][&language]
```

The parameter maxCandidates specifies the number of descriptions to return. The default is 1. The default language is English.

Following is the JSON returned for the image of the three cats used earlier in this chapter:

```
"description": {

"tags": ["cat", "sitting", "wall", "white", "indoor", "black", "sink", "counter",
"domestic cat"],

"captions": [{ "text": "a group of cats sitting on a counter top",   "confidence":
0.6282602548599243  }]  },
```

There are multiple tags related to the content in the image and a single sentence describing the image with a confidence of 62.8%.

Detect objects

The detect operation detects objects in an image and provides coordinates for each object detected. The objects are categorized using an 86-category taxonomy for common objects.

The request URL is formulated as follows:

```
https://{endpoint}/vision/v3.1/detect
```

Following is the JSON returned for the image of the three cats used earlier in this chapter:

```
"objects": [{

"rectangle": {   "x": 556,   "y": 130,   "w": 190,   "h": 277   },   "object": "cat",
"confidence": 0.853,   "parent": {   "object": "mammal",   "confidence": 0.864,
"parent": {   "object": "animal",   "confidence": 0.865   }   } }, {

"rectangle": {   "x": 17,   "y": 183,   "w": 200,   "h": 216   },   "object": "cat",
"confidence": 0.831,   "parent": {   "object": "mammal",   "confidence": 0.839,
"parent": {   "object": "animal",   "confidence": 0.84   }   } }, {

"rectangle": {   "x": 356,   "y": 238,   "w": 182,   "h": 149   },   "object":
"cat",   "confidence": 0.81,   "parent": {   "object": "mammal",   "confidence": 0.816,
"parent": {   "object": "animal",   "confidence": 0.818   }   } }]
```

The detect operation identified three cats with a high level of confidence and provided the coordinates for each cat.

Content tags

The tag operation generates a list of tags, based on the image and the objects in the image. Tags are based on objects, people, and animals in the image, along with the placing of the scene (setting) in the image.

The tags are provided as a simple list with confidence levels.

The request URL is formulated as follows:

```
https://{endpoint}/vision/v3.1/tag[?language]
```

Following is the JSON returned for the image of the three cats used earlier in this chapter:

```
"tags": [{

"name": "cat",   "confidence": 0.9999970197677612   }, {

"name": "sitting",   "confidence": 0.9983036518096924   }, {

"name": "wall",   "confidence": 0.9743844270706177   }, {

"name": "animal",   "confidence": 0.9706938862800598   }, {

"name": "white",   "confidence": 0.9519104957580566   }, {

"name": "indoor",   "confidence": 0.9119423627853394   }, {

"name": "black",   "confidence": 0.8455044031143188   }, {
```

"name": "kitty",   "confidence": 0.8295007944107056 }, {

"name": "small to medium-sized cats",   "confidence": 0.65200275182724 }, {

"name": "sink",   "confidence": 0.6215651035308838 }, {

"name": "feline",   "confidence": 0.5373185276985168 }, {

"name": "counter",   "confidence": 0.51436448097229 }, {

"name": "domestic cat",   "confidence": 0.2866966426372528 }],

The tag operation generated a list of tags in order of confidence. The cat tag has the highest confidence score of 99.9%, with domestic cat the lowest score of 28.7%.

Domain-specific content

There are two models in Computer Vision that have been trained on specific sets of images:

- **Celebrity**   Recognizes famous people.
- **Landmark**   Recognizes famous buildings or outdoor scenery.

The request URL is formulated as follows:

```
https://{endpoint}/vision/v3.1/models/{model}/analyze[?language]
```

The model is either celebrities or landmarks. English is the default language.

Figure 3-8 is a photograph of the Belém tower in Lisbon, Portugal. This is a famous sixteenth-century landmark, the place from where explorers set sail.

FIGURE 3-8 Example of a landmark

The JSON returned includes the name of the celebrity or landmark, as shown next:

```
"landmarks": [{  "name": "Belém Tower",  "confidence": 0.9996672868728638  }]
```

These domain-specific models can also be used by the analyze operations by using the details parameter.

The analyze operation can also detect commercial brands from images using a database of thousands of company and product logos.

Thumbnail generation

The Get thumbnail operation generates a thumbnail image by analyzing the image, identifying the area of interest, and smart crops the image.

The generated thumbnail will differ depending on the parameters you specify for height, width, and smart cropping.

The request URL is formulated as follows:

```
https://{endpoint}/vision/v3.1/generateThumbnail[?width][&height][&smartCropping]
```

Width and height are numeric values. SmartCropping is either 0 or 1.

The response contains a binary jpg image.

Optical character recognition (OCR)

OCR is the extraction of printed or handwritten text from images. You can extract text from images and documents.

There are two operations for extracting text from images:

- **Read**   The latest text recognition model that can be used with images and PDF documents. Read works asynchronously and must be used with the Get Read Results operation.

- **OCR**   An older text recognition model that supports only images and can only be used synchronously.

The request URL for the Read operation is formulated as follows:

```
https://{endpoint}/vision/v3.1/read/analyze[?language]
```

The request URL for the OCR operation is formulated as follows:

```
https://{endpoint}/vision/v3.1/ocr[?language][&detectOrientation]
```

The default language is unknown, and the language will be detected from the text.

Figure 3-9 is an image containing a quote from the Greek philosopher Democritus.

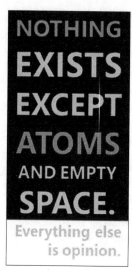

FIGURE 3-9 Quote printed in an image

The JSON returned includes the pieces of text from the image, as shown next:

```
{  "language": "en",  "textAngle": 0.0,  "orientation": "Up",

  "regions": [{

"boundingBox": "21,16,304,451",  "lines": [{  "boundingBox": "28,16,288,41",
"words": [{

"boundingBox": "28,16,288,41",  "text": "NOTHING"  }]  }, {

"boundingBox": "27,66,283,52",  "words": [{  "boundingBox": "27,66,283,52",  "text":
"EXISTS"  }]  }, {

"boundingBox": "27,128,292,49",  "words": [{  "boundingBox": "27,128,292,49",
"text": "EXCEPT"  }]  }, {

"boundingBox": "24,188,292,54",  "words": [{  "boundingBox": "24,188,292,54",
"text": "ATOMS"  }]  }, {

"boundingBox": "22,253,297,32",  "words": [{  "boundingBox": "22,253,105,32",
"text": "AND"  }, {

"boundingBox": "144,253,175,32",  "text": "EMPTY"  }]  }, {

"boundingBox": "21,298,304,60",  "words": [{  "boundingBox": "21,298,304,60",
"text": "SPACE."  }]  }, {

"boundingBox": "26,387,294,37",  "words": [{  "boundingBox": "26,387,210,37",
"text": "Everything"  }, {

"boundingBox": "249,389,71,27",  "text": "else"  }]  }, {
```

```
"boundingBox": "127,431,198,36",    "words": [{    "boundingBox": "127,431,31,29",
"text": "is"    }, {

"boundingBox": "172,431,153,36",    "text": "opinion."    }]    }]    }]
}
```

OCR only extracts the text it identifies. It does not provide any context to the text it extracts. The results are simply pieces of text.

Content moderation

The analyze operation can identify images that are risky or inappropriate. The Content Moderator service, although not part of Computer Vision (it is in the Decision group of APIs), is closely related to it.

Content Moderator is used in social media platforms to moderate messages and images. Content Moderator can be used in education to filter content not suitable for minors.

Content Moderator includes the ability to detect and moderate:

- **Images**   Scans images for adult or racy content, detects text in images with OCR, and detects faces.
- **Text**   Scans text for offensive or sexual content, profanity (in more than 100 languages), and personally identifiable information (PII).
- **Video**   Scans videos for adult or racy content.
- **Custom terms**   You can supply a set of terms that the Content Moderator can use to block or allow.
- **Custom images**   You can supply a set of custom images that the Content Moderator can use to block or allow.

Content Moderator includes a human review tool, a web portal where content that has been identified by the algorithms can be approved or rejected.

Understand the Custom Vision service

The Custom Vision service is an alternative to the pretrained Computer Vision service. Custom Vision enables you to build, train, and deploy a custom image recognition model based on images you provide.

In Custom Vision, you define the labels for your model and a set of sample images. You tag your images with your labels. The Custom Vision service uses a machine learning algorithm to analyze these sample images. Custom Vision trains and evaluates the custom model.

You can then deploy your model with an endpoint and key and consume this model in your apps in a similar way to the Computer Vision service.

Custom Vision supports two different types of mode:

- **Image classification**   Tags an image using the labels defined for the model.
- **Object detection**   Identifies objects using the tags and provides the coordinates of objects in an image. Object detection is a type of classification model.

A model can only be built for one of these two types.

Custom Vision uses a web portal (https://www.customvision.ai) where you can create your model, upload your images, label the images or the objects, train the model, test and evaluate the model, and finally deploy the model.

To use Custom Vision, you will need to create either a Cognitive Services multi-service resource, or a Custom Vision service resource, as described earlier in this chapter. There are two Custom Vision services: Training and Prediction. You will require both services.

Creating a Custom Vision model

The process for creating a Custom Vision model is as follows:

1. Specify the model type.
2. Upload own images.
3. Define your labels.
4. Either
   a. Label images.
   b. Identify the object in the images.
5. Train the model.
6. Evaluate the model.
7. Deploy the model.

Custom Vision exercise

The following steps take you through creating a custom object detection model to identify fruit from images.

We will use the fruits dataset that you can download from https://aka.ms/fruit-objects. Extract the image files. There are 33 images, as shown in Figure 3-10.

You will need to use 30 of the images to train your model, so keep three images for testing your model after you have trained it.

First, you need to create a Custom Vision service. Figure 3-11 shows the pane in the Azure portal for creating a Custom Vision service.

There is a toggle to choose which service(s) you require: Training and/or Prediction. You will need to select the subscription and resource group. You will then need to create a unique name for the service. This name will be the domain name for your endpoint and must be unique worldwide. For the Training resource, you should select the region where the Training resource is to be deployed and select your pricing tier: Free F0 or Standard S0. You then need to select the region and pricing tier for the Prediction resource.

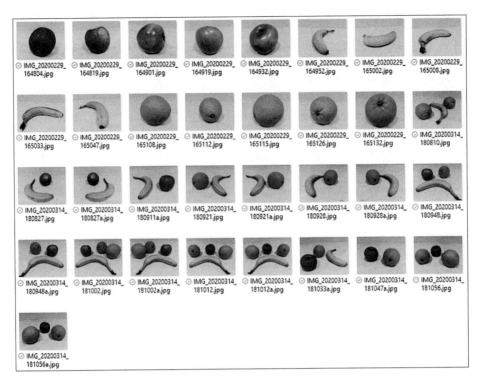

FIGURE 3-10 Images of fruit

FIGURE 3-11 Creating a Cognitive Services resource

Clicking on Review +Create will validate the options. You then click on Create to create the resource. If you selected Both, two resources will be deployed with the Training resource using the name you provided and the name of the Prediction resource with "-Prediction" appended.

You can create Custom Vision resources using the CLI as follows:

```
az cognitiveservices account create --name <unique name for training> --resource-group
<resource group name> --kind CustomVision.Training --sku F0 --location <region>

az cognitiveservices account create --name <unique name for prediction> --resource-group
<resource group name> --kind CustomVision.Prediction --sku F0 --location <region>
```

Next, you need to navigate to the Custom Vision web portal, https://www.customvision.ai, and sign in with the credentials for your Azure subscription.

You will need to create a new project. You will need to name your project and select your Custom Vision training resource (or you can use a multi-service Cognitive Service resource).

Next, you should select Object Detection as the Project Type and General for the Domain, as shown in Figure 3-12.

FIGURE 3-12 New Custom Vision project

The domain is used to train the model. You should select the most relevant domain that matches your scenario. You should use the General domain if none of the domains are applicable.

Domains for image classification are as follows:

- General
- Food
- Landmarks
- Retail
- General (compact)
- Food (compact)
- Landmarks (compact)
- Retail (compact)
- General [A1]
- General (compact) [S1]

Domains for object detection are as follows:

- General
- Logo
- Products on Shelves
- General (compact)
- General (compact) [S1]
- General [A1]

Compact domains are lightweight models that are designed to run locally—for example, on mobile platforms.

NEED MORE REVIEW? DOMAINS

For more explanation as to which domain to choose, see https://docs.microsoft.com/azure/cognitive-services/custom-vision-service/select-domain.

Once the project is created, you should create your tags. In this exercise, you will create three tags:

- Apple
- Banana
- Orange

Next, you should upload your training images. Figure 3-13 shows the Custom Vision project with the images uploaded and untagged.

You now need to click on each image. Custom Vision will attempt to identify objects and highlight the object with a box. You can adjust and resize the box and then tag the objects in the image, as shown in Figure 3-14.

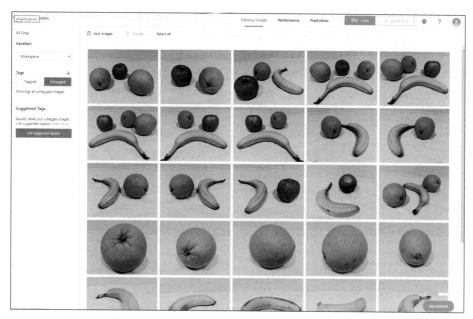

FIGURE 3-13 Custom Vision project with uploaded images

FIGURE 3-14 Tagging objects

You will repeat tagging the objects for all the training images.

You will need at least 10 images for each tag, but for better performance, you should have a minimum of 30 images. To train your model, you should have a variety of images with different lighting, orientation, sizes, and backgrounds.

Select the Tagged button in the left-hand pane to see your tagged images.

You are now ready to train your model. Click on the Train button at the top of the project window. There are two choices:

- **Quick Training**   Training will take a few minutes.
- **Advanced Training**   Specifies the amount of time to spend training the model from 1 to 24 hours.

Select the Quick Training option and click on Train.

When training has completed, the model's performance is displayed. There are two key measures that indicate the effectiveness of the model:

- **Precision**   The percentage of predictions that the model correctly detected. This is a value between 0 and 1 and is shown as a percentage (the higher the better).
- **Recall**   The percentage of the predictions that the model was correct. This is a value between 0 and 1 and is shown as a percentage (the higher the better).

Figure 3-15 shows the results after training the model.

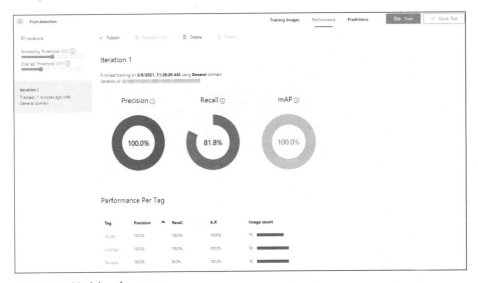

FIGURE 3-15 Model performance

You can use the Quick Test option to check your model. You should upload one of the three images you put aside. The image will be automatically processed, as shown in Figure 3-16.

The model has identified both the apple and the banana and drawn boxes around the pieces of fruit. The objects are tagged, and the results have high confidence scores of 95.2% and 73.7%.

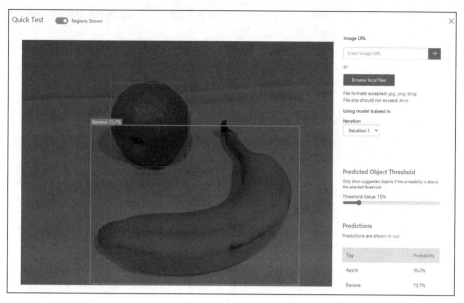

FIGURE 3-16 Quick Test

To publish your model, click on the Publish button at the top of the Performance tab shown in Figure 3-16. You will need to name your model and select a Custom Vision Prediction resource.

> **NOTE PUBLISHED ENDPOINT**
>
> You cannot use a multi-service Cognitive Services resource for the published endpoint.

Publishing will generate an endpoint URL and key so that that your applications can use your custom model.

Computer Vision vs. Custom Vision

It is important that you understand the differences of capabilities of the prebuilt Computer Vision service compared with the capabilities of Custom Vision.

Computer Vision uses prebuilt models trained with many thousands of images. The Computer Vision service has the following capabilities:

- Object detection
- Image classification
- Content moderation
- Optical character recognition (OCR)
- Facial recognition
- Landmark recognition

Custom Vision uses images and tags that you supply to train a custom image recognition model. Custom Vision only has two of the capabilities:

- Object detection
- Image classification

Understand the Face service

While the Computer Vision service includes face detection, it provides only basic information about the person. The Face service performs more detailed analysis of the faces in an image. The Face service can examine facial characteristics, compare faces, and even verify a person's identity. If you want to do analysis around the characteristics of faces or compare faces, you should use the Face service instead of Computer Vision.

Facial recognition has many use cases, such as security, retail, aiding visually challenged people, disease diagnosis, school attendance, and safety.

The Face service contains several advanced face algorithms, enabling face attribute detection and recognition. The Face service examines facial landmarks including noses, eyes, and lips to detect and recognize faces.

The Face service can detect attributes of the face, such as the following:

- Gender
- Age
- Emotions

The Face service can perform facial recognition:

- Similarity matching
- Identity verification

The Face service can be deployed in the Azure portal by searching for Face when creating a new resource. You must select your region, resource group, provide a unique name, and select the pricing tier: Free F0 or Standard S0.

You can create Face resources using the CLI as follows:

```
az cognitiveservices account create --name <unique name> --resource-group <resource
group name> --kind Face --sku F0 --location <region>
```

The Face service has several facial image-processing operations.

Detection

The Face service detects the human faces in an image and returns their boxed coordinates. Face detection extracts face-related attributes, such as head pose, emotion, hair, and glasses.

The Face service examines 27 facial landmarks, as shown in Figure 3-17. The location of eyebrows, eyes, pupils, nose, mouth, and lips are the facial landmarks used by the Face service.

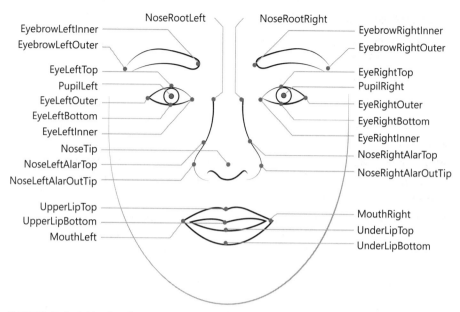

FIGURE 3-17 Facial landmarks

Facial detection provides a set of features, or attributes, about the faces it has detected:

- **Age**   The estimated age in years.
- **Gender**   The estimated gender (male, female, and genderless).
- **Emotion**   A list of emotions (happiness, sadness, neutral, anger, contempt, disgust, surprise, and fear) each with a confidence score. The scores across all emotions add up to 1.
- **Glasses**   Whether the given face has eyeglasses and the type of eye covering (NoGlasses, ReadingGlasses, Sunglasses, or Swimming Goggles).
- **Hair**   Whether the face has hair, and the hair color, or is bald.
- **Facial hair**   Whether the face has facial hair.
- **Makeup**   Whether the eyes and/or lips have makeup as either true or false.
- **Smile**   Whether the face is smiling. A value of 0 means no smile and a value of 1 is a clear smile.
- **Occlusion**   Whether there are objects blocking parts of the face. True or false is returned for eyeOccluded, foreheadOccluded, and mouthOccluded.
- **Blur**   How blurred the face is in the image. This has a value between 0 and 1 with an informal rating of low, medium, or high.
- **Exposure**   The level exposure of the face between 0 and 1 with an informal rating of underExposure, goodExposure, or overExposure.
- **Noise**   The level of visual noise detected in the face image. This has a value between 0 and 1 with an informal rating of low, medium, or high.
- **Head pose**   The orientation of the face. This attribute is described by the pitch, roll, and yaw angles in degrees.

The request URL is formulated as follows:

```
https://{endpoint}/face/v1.0/detect[?returnFaceId][&returnFaceLandmarks]
[&returnFaceAttributes][&recognitionModel][&detectionModel]
```

The parameters you can specify include the following:

- **returnFaceId** True or false to indicate if the API should return IDs of detected faces.
- **returnFaceLandmarks** True or false to indicate if the API should return facial landmarks.
- **returnFaceAttributes** A comma-separated list of the attributes you want returned (age, gender, headPose, smile, facialHair, glasses, emotion, hair, makeup, occlusion, accessories, blur, exposure, and noise).
- **detectionModel** There are three detection models you can use: detection_01, detection_02, and detection_03. The default is detection_01. The detection_02 model should be used for images with small, side, and blurry faces. The detection_03 model has better results on small faces. Facial attributes are not available for detection_02 and detection_03.
- **recognitionModel** You should use the recognitionModel if you want to use the Recognition operations described in the next section. There are three recognition models you can use: recognition_01, recognition_02, and recognition_03. The default model is recognition_01. The latest model, recognition_03, is recommended since its accuracy is higher than the older models.

The detection model returns a FaceId for each face it detects. This Id can then be used by the face recognition operations described in the next section.

The JSON returned using the detect operation on the image of the author in Figure 3-7 is shown next:

```
{   "faceId": "aa2c934e-c0f9-42cd-8024-33ee14ae05af",

 "faceRectangle": {   "top": 613,   "left": 458,   "width": 442,   "height": 442   },

 "faceAttributes": {   "hair": {   "bald": 0.79,   "invisible": false,   "hairColor":
[  {   "color": "gray",   "confidence": 0.98   },  {   "color": "brown",
"confidence": 0.7   },  {   "color": "blond",   "confidence": 0.47   },  {   "color":
"black",   "confidence": 0.45   },  {   "color": "other",   "confidence": 0.28   },
{   "color": "red",   "confidence": 0.04   },  {   "color": "white",   "confidence":
0.0   }  ]   },

 "smile": 0.011,

"headPose": {   "pitch": 2.9,   "roll": -2.2,   "yaw": -9.3   },

 "gender": "male",

 "age": 53.0,

 "facialHair": {   "moustache": 0.9,   "beard": 0.9,   "sideburns": 0.9   },

 "glasses": "ReadingGlasses",
```

"makeup": { "eyeMakeup": false, "lipMakeup": false },

"emotion": { "anger": 0.0, "contempt": 0.0, "disgust": 0.0, "fear": 0.0, "happiness": 0.011, "neutral": 0.989, "sadness": 0.0, "surprise": 0.0 } }

As you can see, the attributes are mainly correct except for the hair color. This is expected as the image in Figure 3-7 was a professionally taken photograph with good exposure and a neutral expression.

Recognition

The Face service can recognize known faces. Recognition can compare two different faces to determine if they are similar (Similarity matching) or belong to the same person (Identity verification).

There are four operations available in facial recognition:

- **Verify**   Evaluates whether two faces belong to the same person. The Verify operation takes two detected faces and determines whether the faces belong to the same person. This operation is used in security scenarios.

- **Identify**   Matches faces to known people in a database. The Identify operation takes one or more face(s) and returns a list of possible matches with a confidence score between 0 and 1. This operation is used for automatic image tagging in photo management software.

- **Find Similar**   Extracts faces that look like a person's face. The Find Similar operation takes a detected face and returns a subset of faces that look similar from a list of faces you supply. This operation is used when searching for a face in a set of images.

- **Group**   Divides a set of faces based on similarities. The Group operation separates a list of faces into smaller groups on the similarities of the faces.

You should not use the Identify or Group operations to evaluate whether two faces belong to the same person. You should use the Verify operation instead.

EXAM TIP

Ensure that you can determine the scenario for each of the four facial recognition operations.

Computer Vision vs. Face service

There are three services that perform an element of facial detection:

- Computer Vision

- Face

- Video Analyzer for Media

It is important that you understand the differences of capabilities of the prebuilt Computer Vision service compared with the capabilities of the Face service and the Video Analyzer for Media service.

Video Analyzer for Media, formerly Video Indexer, is part of Azure Media Services and utilizes Cognitive Services, including the Face service, to extract insights from videos. Video Analyzer for Media can detect and identify people and brands.

EXAM TIP

You will need to be able to distinguish between Computer Vision, Face, and Video Analyzer for Media.

Computer Vision can detect faces in images but can only provide basic information about the person from the image of the face, such as the estimated age and gender.

The Face service can detect faces in images and can also provide information about the characteristics of the face. The Face service can also perform the following:

- Facial analysis
- Face identification
- Pose detection

The Video Analyzer for Media service can detect faces in video images but can also perform face identification.

Here are some examples of the differences between these services:

- The Face API can detect the angle a head is posed at. Computer Vision can detect faces but is not able to supply the angle of the head.
- Video Analyzer for Media can detect faces but does not return the attributes the Face API can return.
- The Face API service is concerned with the details of faces. The Video Analyzer for Media service can detect and identify people and brands but not landmarks.
- Custom Vision allows you to specify the labels for an image. The other services cannot.
- Computer Vision can identify landmarks in an image. The other services cannot.

Understand the Form Recognizer service

Optical character recognition (OCR) is an operation available in Computer Vision. As you will have seen, OCR simply extracts any pieces of text it can find in an image without any context about that text.

The Form Recognizer service extracts text from an image or a document using the context of the document.

NOTE FORM RECOGNIZER

Form Recognizer can extract text, key-value pairs, and tabular data as structured data that can be understood by your application.

Form Recognizer can extract information from scanned forms in images or PDF formats. You can either train a custom model using your own forms or use one of the pre-trained models.

There are three pre-trained models:

- Business cards
- Invoices
- Receipts

The Form Recognizer service can be deployed in the Azure portal by searching for Form Recognizer when creating a new resource. You must select your region, resource group, provide a unique name, and select the pricing tier: Free F0 or Standard S0. The free tier in the Form Recognizer service will only process the first two pages of a PDF document.

You can create Form Recognizer resources using the CLI as follows:

```
az cognitiveservices account create --name <unique name> --resource-group <resource
group name> --kind FormRecognizer --sku F0 --location <region>
```

You can try out the Form Recognizer at https://fott.azurewebsites.net. Figure 3-18 shows a receipt in the Sample labeling tool.

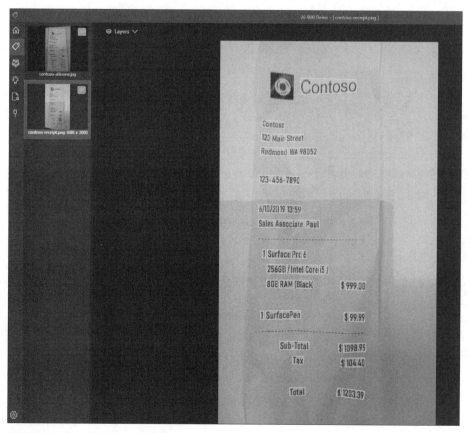

FIGURE 3-18 Form Recognizer tool

The text in the receipt is highlighted in yellow. The information generated from the receipt is as follows:

```
Receipt Type: Itemized

Merchant: Contoso

Address: 123 Main Street Redmond, WA 98052

Phone number: +19876543210

Date: 2019-06-10

Time: 13:59:00

Subtotal: 1098.99

Tax: 104.4

Total: 1203.39

Line items:

Item Quantity: 1

Item Name: Surface Pro 6

Total Price: 999.00

Item Quantity: 1

Item Name: Surface Pen

Total Price: 99.99
```

Form Recognizer vs. OCR

There are three services that perform an element of text extraction from images:

- OCR
- Read
- Form Recognizer

You should understand the differences between these services.

The older OCR operation can only process image files. OCR can only extract simple text strings. OCR can interpret both printed and handwritten text.

The Read operation can process images as well as multi-page PDF documents. Read can interpret both printed and handwritten text.

The Form Recognizer service can extract structured text from images and multi-page PDF documents. Form Recognizer will recognize form fields, and is not just text extraction.

Chapter summary

In this chapter, you learned some of the general concepts related to computer vision. You learned about the types of computer vision, and you learned about the services in Azure Cognitive Services related to computer vision. Here are the key concepts from this chapter:

- Cognitive Services are prebuilt Machine Learning models available through REST APIs.
- Cognitive Services enable applications to see, hear, speak, search, understand, and build intelligence into your applications quickly and easily.
- Cognitive Services can be deployed with either a multi-service resource or single-service resource.
- Cognitive Services can be deployed through the Azure portal or with the CLI.
- You need both the endpoint and key to use an Azure Cognitive Services resource.
- Computer vision analyzes still images and video streams and can detect and classify images.
- Image classification categorizes images based on the content of the image.
- Object detection identifies and tags individual visual features in an image.
- Optical character recognition (OCR) extracts text from an image.
- Facial detection uses the characteristics of a face to provide attributes about the face.
- Computer Vision service can perform many operations on an image. Analyzing the image can detect objects, describe the image in a single sentence, tag the objects in the image, identify brands and landmarks, extract text, and identify inappropriate content.
- Object detection is a type of classification model.
- Custom Vision enables you to build, train, and deploy a custom image recognition model based on images you provide when the prebuilt Computer Vision service does not explain your domain.
- Custom Vision creates a custom image recognition model.
- Custom Vision requires you to upload your images, tag the images, train, and evaluate your model.
- Custom Vision can only perform image classification or object detection.
- Computer Vision service can detect faces in images but only provides basic information about the person and face. The Face service provides more detailed facial analysis.
- The Face service uses facial landmarks to analyze and identify faces.
- The Face service can detect faces and extract attributes about the face.
- The Face service can perform facial recognition.
- Only the Verify operation should be used to identify a person from an image of their face.
- The Form Recognizer service extracts structured contextually aware information from images and documents.

Thought experiment

Let's apply what you have learned in this chapter. In this thought experiment, demonstrate your skills and knowledge of the topics covered in this chapter. You can find the answers in the section that follows.

You work for Fabrikam, Inc., a vehicle insurance company. Fabrikam is interested in processing the many images and documents that customers and assessors send to the company using AI.

Fabrikam wants to evaluate how Cognitive Services can improve their document processing time accuracy.

Fabrikam has recently created an app for customers to send in details of incidents and upload photographs of damage to their vehicles. Fabrikam wants the app to assess the level of damage from the photographs taken.

The app requests that customers take a photo of the driver after an incident. The app also requests that customers take several pictures of the scene of an incident, showing any other vehicles involved and the street. Customers are able upload dashcam videos as evidence for their claims. Customers can also upload scanned images of their claim forms that also contain a diagram explaining the incident.

Insurance adjustors have a mobile app where they can assess and document vehicle damage. Fabrikam wants the app to assess the cost of repairs based on photographs and other information about the vehicle.

Answer the following questions:

1. Assessing the damage to a vehicle from a photograph is an example of which type of computer vision?

2. You need to capture the license plates of the vehicles involved in an incident. Which type of computer vision should you use?

3. You need to confirm that the driver is insured to drive the vehicle. Which type of computer vision should you use?

4. You need to automatically identify the vehicles in the image. Which type of computer vision should you use?

5. Can you use the free tier to create a single resource for all these requirements?

6. You are unable to process some high-quality photographs that customers upload. Can you configure Computer Vision to process these images?

7. You need to prevent your employees from seeing inappropriate customer uploaded content. Which service should you use?

8. Which service should you use to assess the level of damage to a vehicle from a photograph?

9. Which model type should you use to assess the level of damage?

10. Which service should you use to process the scanned claim detail and diagram that the customer has uploaded?

Thought experiment answers

This section contains the solutions to the thought experiment. Each answer explains why the answer choice is correct.

1. Image classification is a machine learning model that predicts the category, or class, the contents of the image belong to. The categories are the level of damage involved.

2. Optical character recognition (OCR) extracts text from an image. You should use OCR to read the license plate of the vehicle but would not be able to assess the level of damage to the vehicle.

3. Identifying people in an image is an example of facial detection and recognition. Facial detection and recognition can identify people in an image.

4. Object detection will identify and tag the vehicle and may be able to identify the manufacturer and model but will not be able to assess the level of damage to the vehicle.

5. No, you cannot use the free tier with a multi-service resource. You must create resources for each Computer Vision service if you want to use the free tier.

6. No, the Computer Vision service only supports file sizes less than 4MB.

7. The Content Moderator service detects potentially offensive or undesirable content from both still images and video content. The Content Moderator provides a review tool where users can examine flagged content and approve or reject the content.

8. You should use the Custom Vision service to assess damage. A set of images can be used to train a custom model. A new image can then be categorized using the model. You would train the model with sets of vehicle images with differing levels of damage with categories (tags) that you define. The model will then be able to place any new image in one of the categories.

9. You should use the image classification model type rather than object detection. Image classification categorizes the images.

10. You should use the Form Recognizer service. This service can process both images and documents and is able to match form fields to data items, extracting the data in a structured format that your application can process.

CHAPTER 4

Describe features of Natural Language Processing (NLP) workloads on Azure

Natural Language Processing (NLP) is the processing of text and speech to extract meaning. NLP can interpret written text and spoken audio and provide detail and understanding about the language used in a computer-readable form.

Natural Language Processing services are provided by Azure Cognitive Services. The concepts involved in NLP will be outlined with use cases, followed by how to use the various Azure Cognitive Services language services.

Language has been a major focus for AI. For many organizations, processing is centered around text and documents and there are large gains to be made by applying AI. There are large amounts of text held in computer-readable formats that can be used to train models. AI can assist users in handling a significant volume of text data and audio streams. For instance, AI can:

- Mine text for patterns and trends.

- Transform unstructured text into more structured formats.

- Generate medical codes by analyzing healthcare documents for specific phrases and terms.

- Sift social media, blog feeds, and webpages to monitor trends.

- Interpret requests and decide on the best action to take—for example, digital assistants.

- Translate text from one language into other languages.

This chapter describes the prebuilt language-related AI capabilities provided by Azure Cognitive Services and explains how to use these language services.

Skills covered in this chapter:

- Skill 4.1: Identify features of common NLP workload scenarios
- Skill 4.2: Identify Azure tools and services for NLP workloads

Skill 4.1: Identify features of common NLP workload scenarios

Natural Language Processing is concerned with understanding written and spoken language. There are countless scenarios for using NLP in applications for organizations across many industries.

A human being can instinctively read and understand the meaning of a piece of unstructured text. NLP does not understand the text in the same way as a human; NLP is the process of gaining insights into text and extracting some meaning from that text.

A major aspect of the Microsoft Azure AI Fundamentals certification is on the capabilities and features of Natural Language Processing and how language services can be applied in different scenarios. This requires you to understand the use cases for Natural Language Processing and to be able to differentiate the various language services in Microsoft Azure.

This skill covers how to:

- Describe Natural Language Processing
- Describe language modeling
- Describe key phrase extraction
- Describe named entity recognition
- Describe sentiment analysis
- Describe speech recognition and synthesis
- Describe translation

Describe Natural Language Processing

Natural Language Processing (NLP) is the process of applying AI algorithms and models to text in documents, email messages, and other sources, as well as to speech to extract attributes about the text and gain insights from the text.

NLP can be used to classify documents or summarize documents by identifying the subjects in the document. The output of NLP can be used for further text-based processing or searching.

NLP can extract key phrases from a document. NLP can recognize questions and intent from text and extract those into requests and actions. NLP can perform sentiment analysis on a document to decide how positively or negatively the language is used.

NLP can interpret spoken language and synthesize speech responses.

EXAM TIP

You need to be able to map the NLP workloads on the scenarios presented or identify which type of NLP workload applies to the requirements described.

Text Analytics techniques

NLP is concerned with applying the following processing techniques to extract meaning and gain insights:

- Analysis of text
  - **Tokenize** Splitting text into words and phrases.
  - **Statistical** Analyzing the terms used, including the frequency of the appearance of individual words.
  - **Frequency** As well as the frequency of individual words, identifying the frequency of phrases.
  - **PosTag (Part of speech tagging)** Assigning parts of speech (noun, verb, or adjective) to each word.
  - **Sentiment analysis** Scoring the text for sentiment, as having a positive or negative feeling.
  - **Language detection** Detecting the predominate language used in the text.
- Language modeling
  - **Semantic modeling** Identifying the relationships between words.
  - **Named entity recognition (NER)** Identifying objects (places, dates, or quantities) in the text.
  - **Topic detection** Combining entities into topics to describe the important topics present in the text.
- Analysis of speech
  - **Conversion of audio into text** Analyzing and interpreting speech and converting into text.
  - **Conversion of text into audio** Analyzing text, identifying phrases, and synthesizing those phrases into spoken audio.
- Translation
  - Automatic translation between languages for both text and speech.

Figure 4-1 shows a screenshot of the Immersive Reader tool. This demonstrates the use of speech tagging. Each word is identified with a tag (adjective, noun, or verb) and is color coded.

FIGURE 4-1 Immersive Reader

Use cases for NLP

There are many use cases for NLP. Some examples are listed next.

A company can search for terms in documents related to their products. For instance, a patent attorney could use NLP to look for examples of prior use when evaluating new patents, or to protect their existing patents by searching for terms in their patents against patents submitted by others.

An organization can monitor social media posts for sentiment and then flag negative sentiment. An example would be an airline that monitors Twitter for posts that mention the airline's name. Any negative tweet can be flagged, and the follower count of the poster used to determine the level of response required.

A call center can use NLP to analyze phone calls. NLP can transcribe the call and identify which voice is speaking.

Organizations can classify emails in customer support. Emails can be prioritized for the urgency of response, if the email is SPAM, or even if an email requires a response at all.

Now, we will examine the major NLP workloads.

Describe language modeling

A common use of NLP is having conversations with humans through chatbots and personal digital assistants. To enable computers to have human-like interactions such as these requires the computer to interpret the meaning of the text supplied, understand what is being requested, and what the request is about.

> **NOTE LANGUAGE MODEL**
>
> A language model is a core component in NLP. The language model uses the statistical techniques described previously to analyze the structures and patterns in text. For instance, a language model will look at the probability of a sequence of words. This is more than extracting the nouns and verbs in a sentence. It is having a model of the language to be able to understand the text supplied. It is more than rules for grammar; humans do not always follow the complex rules for grammar, and these rules vary over time and context.

Language models have been trained to learn the structure of a language by analyzing enormous amounts of text. Language modeling aims to interpret the intent from a text statement and extract key information to discover the overall meaning from the text.

Language modeling is at the heart of creating NLP-based solutions and forms the basis for the other workloads described in this section. Converting a command into smart actions is an example of language modeling. Language modeling interprets the purpose of a text command and turns that command into an intent that can be converted into a smart action for a device to run.

Language modeling does not detect the language in which the text is written. Detecting the language that the text is written in is language detection, not language modeling. Language modeling can be performed in many languages but only one language at a time. Similarly, language modeling does not determine the emotion in a text statement. Determining the emotion in a text statement is sentiment analysis, not language modeling.

Describe key phrase extraction

Key phrase extraction is the evaluation of a piece of text to identify the main talking points, or popular mentions, contained in the text. Key phrase extraction returns a list of talking points. Each talking point is normally a single word or a short phrase.

An example use for key phrase extraction is for website reviews. You can extract key phrases from all the reviews and then add these elements as tags to allow other website users to filter reviews. For example, for the review text, "The food was delicious and there were wonderful staff," the key phrase extraction returns the talking points: "food" and "wonderful staff."

Describe named entity recognition

Named entity recognition (NER) is the identification of entities in a piece of text. Entities are of a type, or class (such as people, places, organizations, numbers, or personal information), and are objects that are already known by the AI workload. Some entities like dates have sub-types, such as time or duration.

Following are common entities available with NER:

- People
- Places
- Organizations
- Dates and times
- Date
- Duration
- Time
- Quantities
- Age
- Temperature

NER can also find personal information including email addresses, telephone numbers, social security numbers, driver license numbers, and passport numbers.

NER can be used to extract brand information in emails and social media posts. You can use NER to find mentions of your product names. For example, the Content Moderator service uses NER to scan text against a list of terms that you have provided.

You can use NER to scan news feeds for mentions of people or organizations and tag those documents. For example, you can create a curated list of daily news articles that are relevant to your company or clients.

Describe sentiment analysis

A common use for NLP is to score text for sentiment. *Sentiment analysis* is the determination if a piece of text has a positive or negative feeling or emotion.

Sentiment analysis can be used to listen to what customers think of your products and services by analyzing social media for positive or negative sentiment. There are many third-party applications—for example, Hootsuite—that monitor and track social media using sentiment analysis, allowing you to monitor trends and to take action.

Describe speech recognition and synthesis

NLP is not just for text; it includes the spoken word. Speech covers both *speech recognition*, detecting and interpreting spoken input and converting into text, and *speech synthesis*, generating spoken output from text.

Speech recognition

Speech recognition does not simply recognize words; it must find patterns in the audio. Speech recognition uses an acoustic language model that converts the audio into phonemes. A *phoneme* is the smallest unit of sound in speech. When we teach children to read, we teach how letters are represented by sounds. In English, however, there are 26 letters in the alphabet, but there are 44 phonemes, and similar words can be pronounced very differently.

The baked good, scone, is an example of the different phonemes. Scone has two common pronunciations in England: one that rhymes with "cone" and another that rhymes with "gone." If you are in Scotland, you might hear it pronounced as "skoon."

Once the phonemes have been identified, the acoustic model then maps phonemes to words, using statistical algorithms that predict the most probable sequence of words based on the phonemes.

An example of speech recognition can be found in Microsoft PowerPoint. The Presenter Coach tool monitors your speech and uses speech recognition to give you a statistical report for a rehearsal of your presentation. It will tell you if you have used filler words or euphemisms, and it detects if you are just reading the text from the slide. It will also provide suggestions to improve your delivery.

Other common NLP scenarios for speech recognition include interactive voice response in call centers, transcribing telephone calls, and in-home automation.

Speech synthesis

Synthesized speech does not generate a sound for each word. It converts the text into phrases, and then using the acoustic model, converts the phrases into smaller prosodic units and then into phonemes.

A voice is then applied to convert the phonemes into audio speech. The voice defines the pitch, speaking rate, and intonation for the generated audio.

You find speech synthesis in personal digital assistants, like Siri and Cortana, that respond vocally to your requests.

Common NLP scenarios for speech synthesis are broadcasting arrivals and departures at airports, reading out text messages while you are driving your car, and screen reading software applications for visually impaired people.

Describe translation

There are many languages in the world, and the ability to convert text from one language into another language is a feature of NLP.

Translation is very difficult for humans to do. Disclaimer: My wife is a translator from Italian to English. Languages do not have simple word-for-word translations; for instance, there are words in Italian that can be one of multiple words in English, depending on the context. There are Italian words that do not have a simple translation, such as Ciofeca, which means a poor quality and badly prepared drink, such as coffee. Another example is *volume* in Italian means the space inside an object, whereas *volume* in English generally is a measurement of that space. *Volume* can also refer to the level of sound, or a book in a series. The German word, Schaden-freude, has no direct translation and generally means to derive pleasure from someone else's misfortune. In Finnish, the word Kalsarikännit means the feeling you get when sitting at home getting drunk in your underwear. As you can see, translation is hard and relies on context and a lot of knowledge.

Most human translators translate from one language into their native language; they do not translate the other way around, as they need to make the text understandable to the native speaker. You have probably all seen instruction manuals poorly translated where a native speaker has not been used.

To translate from one language to another requires models for both languages and to be able to understand the context of how each language is used. This involves understanding rules of grammar, use of informal language, and large dictionaries and glossaries.

AI-powered text translation uses large amounts of translated text to train the translation models. You will find that the translations are better where there are more examples of the text available in each language, so the results of translation between English and other languages are often better than translation between other languages. Translation results tend to be better on news and marketing documents than on highly technical documents, as again, there are more examples of the former available to train the models on.

Translation includes the conversion of both text and audio speech from one language into another:

- **Text** Text translation translates the text documents from one language to another language.
- **Speech** Speech translation translates spoken audio from one language to another language.

Now that we have explained the common NLP workloads, we will look at the services in Azure Cognitive Services for the major NLP workloads.

Skill 4.2: Identify Azure tools and services for NLP workloads

Azure Cognitive Services provides pre-trained NLP models that cover most of the capabilities required for analyzing text and speech. This section describes the capabilities of the main language services within Azure Cognitive Services.

These language services allow developers to add features such as sentiment detection, speech recognition, and language understanding to their applications without needing skills in machine learning. These language services are available for both text and speech.

The text services extract meaning from unstructured text:

- **Text Analytics** Discovers insights from textual data. Text Analytics is one of the most heavily used Cognitive Services.
- **Language Understanding service (LUIS)** Interprets the intent and extracts key information from supplied text. LUIS is used by other Cognitive Services to provide understanding of text.
- **Translator** Detects and translates text in real time, or in batch, across more than 90 languages.
- **Immersive Reader** Helps readers of all ages and abilities to comprehend text using audio and visual cues.
- **QnA Maker** Creates a question-and-answer knowledge base from existing documents and sources. QnA Maker is explained in Chapter 5.

The speech services allow you to add speech processing into your apps:

- **Speech to Text** Transcribes audio into text in real time or from audio files.
- **Text to Speech** Synthesizes text into spoken audio.
- **Speech Translation** Converts audio into text and translates into another language in real time. Speech Translation leverages the Translator service.
- **Speaker Recognition** Identifies people from the voices in an audio clip.

The Microsoft Azure AI Fundamentals certification encompasses the capabilities of Natural Language Processing services. This requires you to understand the capabilities of the services described in this section.

> **This skill covers how to:**
> - Identify the capabilities of the Text Analytics service
> - Identify the capabilities of the Language Understanding service (LUIS)
> - Identify the capabilities of the Speech service
> - Identify the capabilities of the Translator service

EXAM TIP

You need to be able to map the service to the scenario presented and to identify the operation for a service to use.

Language services are used alongside other Cognitive Services, such as OCR and Content Moderation described in Chapter 3, and with bots described in Chapter 5.

To use the language services, you will need to create a Cognitive Services multi-service resource, or a language single-service resource, as described in Chapter 3.

The following sections describe the capabilities of four of the main language APIs provided by Cognitive Services.

Identify the capabilities of the Text Analytics service

The Text Analytics service is an Azure Cognitive Service that performs a series of Natural Language Processing operations on text.

Text Analytics can detect the sentiment of sentences or whole paragraphs. You can extract key phrases from a piece of text, and extract entities such as people, places, and things from a piece of text.

You can see how Text Analytics works without an Azure subscription at https://azure. microsoft.com/services/cognitive-services/text-analytics/, as shown in Figure 4-2. The text for a restaurant review is analyzed, and the results are presented both in a friendly format and in JSON format.

The Text Analytics service can be deployed in the Azure portal by searching for Text Analytics when creating a new resource. You must select your region, select the resource group, provide a unique name, and select the pricing tier: Free F0 or Standard.

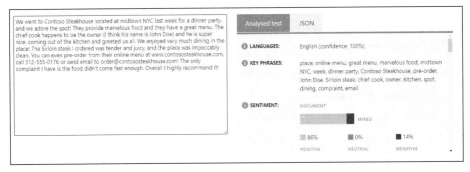

FIGURE 4-2 Text Analytics

You can create Text Analytics resources using the CLI, as follows:

```
az cognitiveservices account create --name <unique name> --resource-group <resource
group name> --kind TextAnalytics --sku F0 --location <region>
```

The following sections describe the capabilities of the operations available with the Text Analytics service.

Detect language

Text Analytics supports a wide range of languages. A key operation is the identification of the language used in a document. Text Analytics can detect a wide range of languages, variants, dialects, and some regional/cultural languages—for example, French (fr-Fr) vs. Canadian French (fr-CA).

The Detect language operation returns the name of the language, the ISO language code, and a level of confidence between 0 and 1. If there is more than one language in the document, then the predominant language is returned.

The request URL is formulated as follows:

```
https://{endpoint}/text/analytics/v3.0/languages
```

You supply a JSON document containing text to be analyzed. Following is the JSON returned for the paragraph on translation from earlier in the chapter that has a mixture of English, German, Italian, and Finnish words:

```
"documents": [

{ "id": "1", "detectedLanguage":

{ "name": "English", "iso6391Name": "en", "confidenceScore": 1.0 },
```

This operation found that the language was English, an ISO code "en," with a confidence score of 100%.

Sentiment analysis

Sentiment analysis analyzes the emotion for each sentence in a piece of text and for the whole document.

Sentiment is a classification model that evaluates the emotion of the text as to how positive or negative it is. The operation returns a sentiment score between 0 and 1, with 1 as the most positive, and a sentiment label (positive, negative, neutral, or mixed).

Sentiment analysis uses a model that has been pre-trained on millions of examples of text. Currently, sentiment can be evaluated for 13 languages.

The request URL is formulated as follows:

```
https://{endpoint}/text/analytics/v3.0/sentiment
```

You supply a JSON document containing text to be analyzed. Following is the JSON returned for parts of the paragraph on translation from earlier in this chapter:

```
"documents": [{ "id": "1",

"sentiment": "mixed", "confidenceScores": { "positive": 0.31, "neutral": 0.01,
"negative": 0.68 },

"sentences": [

{ "sentiment": "negative", "confidenceScores": { "positive": 0.0, "neutral": 0.0,
"negative": 1.0 }, "offset": 0, "length": 47, "text": "Translation is very difficult for
humans to do." },

{ "sentiment": "negative", "confidenceScores": { "positive": 0.0, "neutral": 0.0,
"negative": 1.0 }, "offset": 48, "length": 65, "text": "Translation is hard and relies
on context and a lot of knowledge." },

{ "sentiment": "positive", "confidenceScores": { "positive": 0.93, "neutral": 0.03,
"negative": 0.04 }, "offset": 114, "length": 37, "text": "Luckily, Cognitive Services
can help" }]
```

This operation found that the overall sentiment of the paragraph is mixed with a positive score of 31% and a negative score of 68%. The first and second sentences are 100% negative, while the third sentence is 93% positive.

Key phrase extraction

Key phrase extraction identifies the main talking points in unstructured text. The operation generates a list of relevant words and/or phrases that describes the subject of the document. It should be noted that the phrases are returned as a simple list without any context.

Key phrase extraction uses a model that has been pre-trained on millions of examples of text. Currently, phrases can be extracted for 16 languages.

The request URL is formulated as follows:

```
https://{endpoint}/text/analytics/v3.0/keyPhrases
```

You supply a JSON document containing text to be analyzed. Following is the JSON returned for parts of the paragraph on translation from earlier in the chapter:

```
"documents": [{ "id": "1", "keyPhrases": ["Translation", "context", "lot of knowledge",
"humans", "Cognitive Services"]}
```

The key phrase extraction operation found five key phrases in the paragraph of text.

Named entity recognition

Named entity recognition extracts a wide set of prebuilt entities from documents. Entities are objects in the text such as people, places, organizations, date/time, numbers, and personally identifiable information (PII).

> **NOTE ENTITY RECOGNITION**
>
> Microsoft has referred to named entity recognition as entity recognition in the past but is now using the more common term in its documentation. In the exam, you may see usage of entity recognition. Named entity recognition and entity recognition refer to the same operation.

The categories of entities extracted by Text Analytics are:

- **Person**   The names of people. This is not limited to famous people but can identify forenames and surnames in the text.
- **PersonType**   The job type or job title.
- **DateTime**   Dates and times of day including durations and date ranges.
- **Quantity**   Numerical measurements and units including temperature, percentages, ages, and dimensions.
- **Location**   A geographical feature, landmark, building, or city.
- **Organization**   The names of companies, political groups, musical bands, sports teams, government bodies, and public organizations.
- **Event**   The names of historical, social, and other events.
- **Product**   Physical objects. Currently these are computing related.
- **Skill**   Capabilities, skills, or expertise.
- **Address**   Addresses including street, city, and postal code.
- **Phone number**   Telephone numbers.
- **Email**   Email addresses.
- **URL**   URLs to websites.
- **IP**   Network IP addresses.

The operation returns the entity, its category, and a confidence score between 0 and 1. Currently, entities can be extracted for 23 languages, including Arabic.

> **NOTE ENTITY LINKING**
>
> Text Analytics also provides links to Wikipedia articles for well-known entities.

The request URL is formulated as follows:

```
https://{endpoint}/text/analytics/v3.0/entities/recognition/general
```

You supply a JSON document containing text to be analyzed. Following is the JSON returned for the parts of the paragraph on translation earlier in the chapter:

```
"documents": [{ "id": "1", "entities": [

{ "text": "Translation", "category": "Skill", "offset": 0, "length": 11,
"confidenceScore": 0.8 },

{ "text": "Azure", "category": "Organization", "subcategory": "Sports", "offset": 123,
"length": 5, "confidenceScore": 0.53 }]
```

Two entities were extracted: Translation as a skill with confidence score of 80% and Azure as a sport organization with a confidence score of 53%. Clearly, this second entity is incorrect.

Linked entities were also identified.

```
"documents": [{ "id": "1", "entities": [

{ "name": "Translation", "matches": [{ "text": "Translation", "offset": 0, "length":
11, "confidenceScore": 0.13 }, { "text": "Translation", "offset": 48, "length": 11,
"confidenceScore": 0.13 }], "language": "en", "id": "Translation", "url": "https://
en.wikipedia.org/wiki/Translation", "dataSource": "Wikipedia" },

{ "name": "Cognitive computing", "matches": [{ "text": "Cognitive Services", "offset":
123, "length": 18, "confidenceScore": 0.76 }], "language": "en", "id": "Cognitive
computing", "url": "https://en.wikipedia.org/wiki/Cognitive_computing", "dataSource":
"Wikipedia" }]
```

Two Wikipedia articles have been identified: one for Translation and the other related to Cognitive Services.

Use cases for Text Analytics

I have implemented solutions for call centers for much of my career using a variety of tools. Call centers require feedback as they need to measure and improve customer satisfaction and evaluate call center agent performance.

Many call centers use feedback tools such as post call surveys and listening to calls manually, which can be both inaccurate and time consuming. We can use Text Analytics to aid staff and managers to gain statistics and insights into telephone calls, as described next:

- First, Speech to Text transcribes call recordings recorded calls to text.
- Voice recognition can be used to break the text into who is speaking in turn.
- Sentiment analysis can analyze the sentiment of each interaction. We can then track:
  - How the customer sentiment changes over the lifetime of the call.
  - If the agent can convert negative exchanges into positive conversations.
- Key phrase extraction can extract the main talking points in the conversation. This can be used to categorize the call.
- Named entity recognition can extract entities such as people's names, company names, locations, dates, and personal information. This data can enhance the data held for the customer.

Another use case for Text Analytics is in handling compliance. You can scan the emails and call recordings made by your sales team to automate compliance checking by scanning for mentions of key phrases or named entities that represent your products and services.

Identify the capabilities of the Language Understanding service (LUIS)

The Language Understanding service (LUIS) is a key component of Azure Cognitive Services and is used by many of the other Cognitive Services. LUIS is a Natural Language Understanding (NLU) service that analyzes user input and uses a language model to understand the meaning of that text input.

A major strength of AI-based solutions is the ability to converse with users using natural language. Chatbots are a common tool that requires language understanding and is one of the major consumers of LUIS. Using LUIS, you can add conversational intelligence into your bot. We will look further at conversational AI in the next chapter.

Fully understanding what a conversation is about is a hard AI problem to solve. LUIS only focuses on identifying the user's intention and extracting information from a small piece of text. LUIS attempts to identify:

- What the user wants.
- What the user is talking about.

LUIS uses language modeling algorithms developed by Microsoft over many years to apply intelligence to a user's natural language text. LUIS uses the techniques outlined earlier in the chapter together with the language model to predict the user's overall meaning and to extract relevant information. Your applications can then use this information to respond intelligently to the user or to carry out the user's instructions.

You can see how LUIS works without an Azure subscription at https://azure.microsoft.com/services/cognitive-services/language-understanding-intelligent-service/#demo, as shown in Figure 4-3. In this demo, you can either type an instruction or pick an example. When you click on Submit, the instruction is evaluated by LUIS, and the action taken is shown in the image.

The phrase "switch floor lamp to green" has been evaluated, and LUIS has identified that the request is to "TurnOn" the "light" on the "floor" and set the "color" to "green."

LUIS is trained to handle common business domains, including customer service, restaurant reservations, and home automation. Unlike the other language services that are pre-trained, you can create models for your own domains if the prebuilt options do not meet your business scenario.

Remote light control

Type a command to control the lights:

switch floor lamp to green | Submit

OR pick one of ours:

| turn the right light on | switch all lights to green | turn on the left light | all on |
| switch floor lamp to green | turn the table light off | all lights off | |

Smart light application in action

LUIS application response ℹ

```
{
  "query": "switch floor lamp to green",
  "topScoringIntent": {
    "intent": "TurnOn",
    "score": 0.9932177
  },
  "entities": [
    {
      "entity": "floor",
      "type": "Light",
      "startIndex": 7,
      "endIndex": 11,
      "resolution": null,
      "score": 0.905927334
    },
    {
      "entity": "green",
      "type": "Color",
      "startIndex": 21,
      "endIndex": 25,
      "resolution": null,
      "score": 0.9996885
    }
  ]
}
```

FIGURE 4-3 LUIS demo

Key concepts

There are three key concepts in LUIS that you need to understand before creating LUIS applications, as follows:

- **Utterances** An *utterance* is an example phrase that a user says. You need to specify sample utterances to train your model.
- **Intents** An *intent* is the action that the user wants to perform. An intent is linked to multiple utterances.
- **Entities** Entities are like the entities in NER. *Entities* are the subjects or context for the intent.

EXAM TIP

Understanding the difference between these concepts is a fundamental skill in this exam.

You first define your intents. Intents are linked to the actions that your client application can perform. You should create an intent when you want to trigger an action in your client application. You then add a few potential utterances to each intent. LUIS then takes these examples of phrases with the intents and starts training the model. These training utterances are used by your LUIS model to determine which intent the user is referring to.

Let's look at an example for intents and utterances. We will use a LUIS model to power a bot that handles requests around creating and using Cognitive Services. Consider this list of intents and associated utterances:

- CreateCognitiveService
  - "I must deploy Cognitive Services"
  - "I want to create a Cognitive Service resource"
  - "I need to generate a new LUIS authoring resource"
  - "Create Azure Cognitive Services"
- CallCognitiveService
  - "I want to evaluate the sentiment for this sentence"
  - "I need to determine which language this text"
  - "I have to translate this document"
  - "What is the best service for extracting text from an image"

LUIS does not have deep sematic Natural Language Processing. For instance, LUIS cannot automatically differentiate different verb tenses or alternative words. As an example, LUIS is unable to determine if the words add, adding, and added have the same intent. LUIS is unable to automatically recognize that the words add, create, and generate have the same intent. Therefore, you need to provide a set of utterances to help LUIS handle the different ways a user might phrase their requests. LUIS has been developed so that you only need to provide a few sample utterances for LUIS to create a model with good accuracy and do not have to provide every possible variation yourself.

When creating utterances, you need to provide different ways of saying the same thing with different verb tenses and substitute wording. Microsoft recommends that you should create between 10 and 30 utterances per intent. The more example utterances you provide, the more accurate your model will be.

You also need intents and utterances for greetings and other non-action phrases that a user might employ.

Entities are the information required to perform the action behind the intent; they are the data for the action. For the previous example, the entities might be:

- Cognitive Services
- LUIS authoring resource
- Resource
- Document
- Sentence
- Text
- Paragraph
- Image

Once you define your utterance and entities, you can improve the accuracy of the language model by adding hints, known as *features*, by providing variations for the words used. LUIS will then use these features when recognizing the intent and entities.

There are prebuilt entities you can use in your model, and you can specify your own custom entities. There are four types of entity you can create:

- **Machine learned** Entities that are learned from your utterances. When you train the model, the entities are identified from the labels you apply to the utterances.

- **List** A simple list of items for exact text matching. You can also supply synonyms. For the example, you could add "Document" to a list with the synonyms "paragraph," "sentence," and "text."

- **Regex** A regular expression—for example, telephone numbers or postal codes—that matches exactly.

- **Pattern** Pattern.any is used where utterances are very similar but refer to different entities. For example, you can use the pattern {Azure service} to extract "Language Understanding" from the utterance "How should I create a Language Understanding resource in the Azure portal."

> ***NOTE* INTENTS VS. UTTERANCES VS. ENTITIES**
>
> An intent is the required outcome from an utterance and is linked to an action. Entities are data in an utterance. Entities are the information needed to perform the action identified in the intent.

Prebuilt models

LUIS contains several prebuilt models. These models provide combinations of intents, utterances, and entities. You can use a prebuilt domain model that contains intents, utterances, and entities, or you can use a prebuilt intent model that contains intents and utterances, or you can use a prebuilt entity model.

The following prebuilt domain models are available in LUIS:

- **Calendar** Making appointments.
- **Communication** Messaging and telephone calls.
- **Email** Reading and replying to emails
- **HomeAutomation** Controlling smart devices.
- **Notes** Taking notes.
- **Places** Organizations, restaurants, and public spaces.
- **RestaurantReservation** Booking tables in a restaurant.
- **ToDo** Managing tasks.
- **Utilities** Common tasks that you can use in any domain.
- **Weather** Weather forecasts.
- **Web** Navigation to websites.

Prebuilt intent models contain intents and utterances but not entities. The intents from the prebuilt domains can also be added without adding the whole domain model.

Prebuilt entities handle many of the common concepts you need for LUIS apps. The following prebuilt entities are available:

- Age
- Currency
- DateTime
- Dimension
- Email
- Geography
- KeyPhrase
- Number
- Ordinal
- Percentage
- PersonName
- Phonenumber
- Temperature
- URL

Custom schema

A *custom schema* consists of intents and, optionally, entities. A new custom schema has no intents or models. You can add any prebuilt domain, intents, and entities to a custom model. You are not just restricted to a single prebuilt model but can add as many as required.

You can, of course, create your own intents, utterances, and entities and combine them with the prebuilt models to create the schema for your LUIS app.

LUIS app

To use LUIS, you will need to create a LUIS app that describes the model for your domain. LUIS requires both an authoring resource and a prediction resource. The authoring resource is used to create, manage, train, test, and publish your applications. The prediction resource is used by other applications after you publish your LUIS application to understand text inputs.

LUIS uses a web portal (https://www.luis.ai) where you can create your model, add example utterances, train the model, and finally deploy the app.

Understanding machine learning is not necessary to use LUIS. Instead, you define the intents and entities and then provide example utterances to LUIS and relate how those utterances are related to intents and entities. LUIS uses this information to train the model. You can improve the model interactively by identifying and correcting prediction errors.

The process for creating a LUIS app is as follows:

- **Build a LUIS schema**   Define the domain and add intents and entities.
- **Add utterances**   Add training example phrases for each intent.
- **Label entities**   Tag the entities in each utterance.
- **Add features**   Create phrase lists for words with similar meanings.
- **Train**   Train the model in the app.
- **Publish**   Publish the app to an endpoint using the prediction resource.
- **Test**   Test your LUIS app using the published endpoint.

Before you can create a LUIS app, you need to create your LUIS resources. You need both an authoring resource and a prediction resource. The rest of this section will walk you through creating LUIS resources and creating a LUIS app.

To create a resource for LUIS resource in the Azure portal, search for Language Understanding and pick the service titled just Language Understanding, as shown in Figure 4-4.

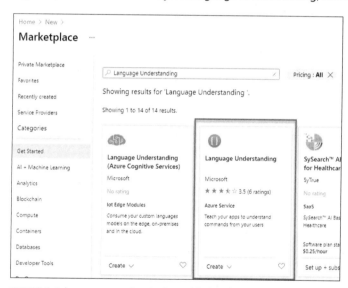

FIGURE 4-4 Language services in Azure Marketplace

Clicking on Create will show the description for the service, as shown in Figure 4-5.

FIGURE 4-5 Service description for the LUIS service

After clicking on the Create button, the Create Language Understanding (LUIS) pane opens, as shown in Figure 4-6.

There is a toggle to choose which service(s) you require: Authoring and/or Prediction. You will need to select your subscription and resource group. You will then need to create a unique name for the service. This name will be the domain name for your endpoints and so must be unique worldwide. For the authoring resource, you should select the region where the authoring resource is to be deployed and select your pricing tier; Free F0 is the only option. You then need to select the region and pricing tier for the prediction resource. The pricing tier for the prediction resource can either be Free F0 or Standard S0.

FIGURE 4-6 Creating LUIS resources

Clicking on Review + Create will validate the options. You then click on Create to create the resource. If you selected Both, two resources will be deployed with the authoring resource using the name you provided appended with "-Authoring" and the prediction resource using the name you provided.

You can create the LUIS resources using the CLI as follows:

```
az cognitiveservices account create --name <unique name for authoring> --resource-group
<resource group name> --kind LUIS.Authoring --sku F0 --location <region>

az cognitiveservices account create --name <unique name for prediction> --resource-group
<resource group name> --kind LUIS --sku F0 --location <region>
```

Once your resources have been created, you will need to obtain the REST API URL and the key to access the resources. To view the endpoint and keys in the Azure portal, navigate to the resource and click on Keys and Endpoint, as shown in Figure 4-7.

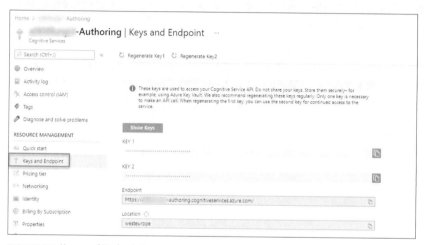

FIGURE 4-7 Keys and Endpoint

Once you have created your LUIS resources, you can open the LUIS web portal (https://www.luis.ai) in a browser. You will be prompted to select your subscription and authoring resource, as shown in Figure 4-8.

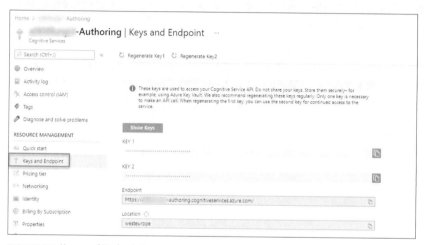

FIGURE 4-8 Selecting the LUIS authoring resource

You then need to click on + New app in the LUIS portal to create a new app. You need to enter a name for the app, select the culture, select the language the app will understand, and choose your prediction resource. If a window appears titled, "How to create an effective LUIS app," you can close this window.

> **NOTE** **LUIS RESOURCES**
>
> There are two resources in a LUIS app: the authoring resource used to build, manage, train, test, and publish your LUIS model, and a prediction resource to query the model. You can use the multi-service Cognitive Services resource for prediction, but you must create an authoring resource in order to create a LUIS app.

You then need to click on + New app in the LUIS portal to create a new app. You must enter a name for the app, select the culture, the language the app will understand, and choose your prediction resource. You will then see the authoring window for your app, as shown in Figure 4-9.

FIGURE 4-9 Authoring LUIS app

Next, you should add prebuilt domains. Click on Prebuilt Domains in the left-hand navigation pane, select the following domains, and click on Add domain:

- Utilities
- Web

Click on Intents in the left-hand navigation pane. You will now see that a number of intents from these domains have been added to your app.

You can now add your own intents. Click + Create, create the following intents, and add the example user inputs (utterances).

- CreateCognitiveService
- CallCognitiveService

For each intent, add example user inputs, with utterances such as the following:

- "I must deploy Cognitive Services"
- "I want to create a Cognitive Service resource"
- "I need to generate a new LUIS authoring resource"
- "Create Azure Cognitive Services"
- "I want to evaluate the sentiment for this sentence"

- "I need to determine which language this text"
- "I have to translate this document"
- "What is the best service for extracting text from an image"

Click on Entities in the left-hand navigation pane. You will see the prebuilt entities already added from the prebuilt domains you selected, as shown in Figure 4-10.

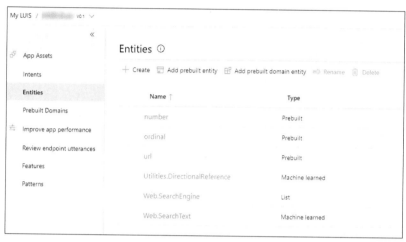

FIGURE 4-10 LUIS entities

Click on the Add prebuilt entity and add the following entities:

- keyPhrase
- personName

Click on the Add prebuilt domain entity and add the Places.product entity.

You can now add your own entities. Click + Create, name your entity AzureServices, and choose the List type. Enter the following values and synonyms:

- Cognitive Services
- Computer Vision
- Custom Vision
- Face
- OCR
- LUIS
- Language Understanding
- Text Analytics
- Sentiment Analysis
- Language Detection
- Translator

You now need to tag the entities in each of the utterances. Edit the CreateCognitiveService intent. Use the mouse to select the name of an Azure service in an utterance. As you select a word or phrase, a window will appear where you can select an entity. Choose the AzureServices entity, as shown in Figure 4-11.

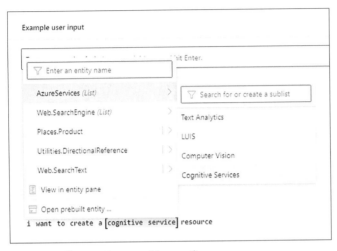

FIGURE 4-11 Tag an utterance with an entity

Edit the CallCognitiveService intent and click on + Add feature. Click on + Create new phrase list. The phrase list should be named TextSources with these values: Document, Paragraph, Sentence, and Text.

The intent will now look similar to Figure 4-12.

You are now ready to train your model. Click on the Train button at the top of the LUIS authoring page. Training will take a few minutes.

The LUIS portal allows you to test your app interactively. Click on the Test button at the top of the LUIS authoring page. A pane will appear where you can enter a test utterance. First try one of the example utterances you add to an intent—for example, "I have to translate this document." You can see the results as shown in Figure 4-13.

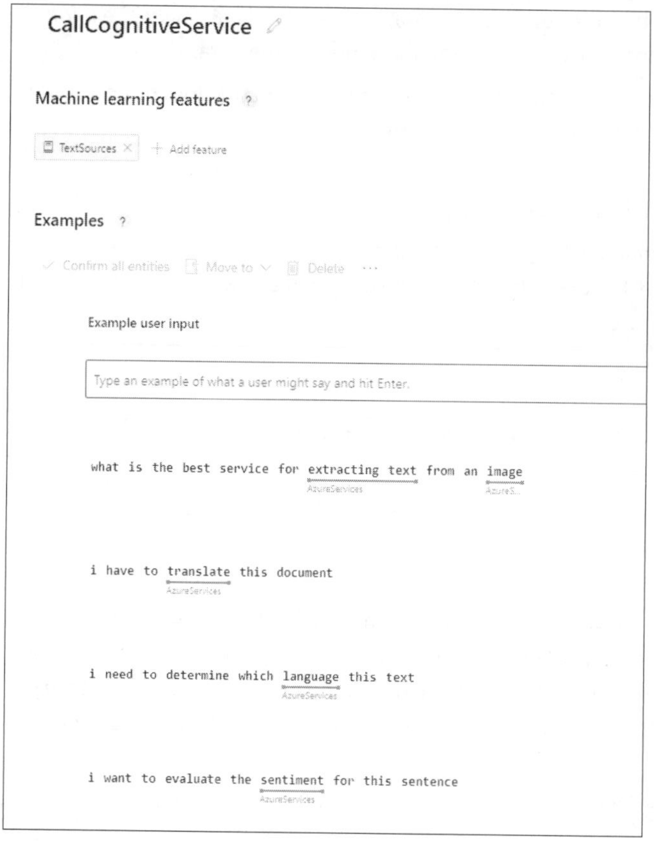

CallCognitiveService ✎

Machine learning features ?

🖳 TextSources ✕   + Add feature

Examples ?

✓ Confirm all entities   ⬚ Move to ⌄   🗑 Delete   ⋯

Example user input

Type an example of what a user might say and hit Enter.

what is the best service for extracting text from an image
                              AzureServices   AzureS...

i have to translate this document
         AzureServices

i need to determine which language this text
                              AzureServices

i want to evaluate the sentiment for this sentence
                       AzureServices

FIGURE 4-12 Intent with tags and features

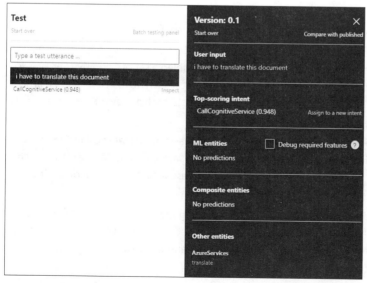

FIGURE 4-13 Test results

You should see in the results the selected intent (action) and entity (data). This is the information that your client application can use to perform the action on the data.

Try other phrases with different wording and evaluate the model. If LUIS does not correctly predict the intent, you can fix this by assigning to the correct intent.

When you have completed the testing of your LUIS app, you can publish the app. After publishing a prediction endpoint URL will be available.

To use a Language Understanding (LUIS) model to find the intent of a text statement in a client application, you need the ID of the LUIS app and the endpoint and key for the prediction resource, not the authoring resource.

Use cases for LUIS

LUIS is not typically used on its own. It is used to provide enhanced user experience in other applications.

For instance, you could create an application that provides a searchable interface for a medical database and document store. You could create a LUIS app with entities for specific medical terminology to help the user find the relevant entries in the database.

Another use is in gaming, where you have the player either issuing verbal or written instructions, in single- and multi-player modes. For example, there a lot of different ways for a player to say, "let's go," especially in stressful situations or when reacting instinctively to the appearance of danger. There is "Get me out of here," "Beam me up," "Engage the warp-drive," and so on.

LUIS can be used with IoT devices to turn a user's command into an action that is understandable by the device.

We will see in the next chapter how LUIS is used with QnA Maker and chatbots.

Identify the capabilities of the Speech service

Speech recognition has long been a goal for AI. After over 15 years of development, it is only recently that algorithms have been developed that have enabled a set of Cognitive Services to be made available for you to use in your applications as a set of easy-to-consume APIs. These APIs are the same ones that Microsoft uses in its own products, such as PowerPoint's live captions and subtitles.

Modern speech recognition technology relies on machine-learned statistical models that leverage cloud computing combined with vast quantities of sample audio. Microsoft's speech recognition technology handles dialects and accents of different speakers; it can deal with jargon, and it performs well in noisy conditions.

The Speech service contains an acoustic model and a language model for many languages. The acoustic model in the Speech service is a deep neural network trained on thousands of hours of audio using advanced algorithms. The number of languages varies by operation and is increasing all the time.

The Speech service can be deployed in the Azure portal by searching for Speech when creating a new resource. You must select your region, select the resource group, provide a unique name, and select the pricing tier: Free F0 or Standard S0. Be careful, and do not create the service called Speech to Text; this is a third-party paid-for service.

You can create Speech resources using the CLI, as follows:

```
az cognitiveservices account create --name <unique name> --resource-group <resource
group name> --kind SpeechServices --sku F0 --location <region>
```

The Speech service has several speech-processing operations.

Speech to Text

The Speech to Text API detects and transcribes spoken input into text. The Speech to Text operation can transcribe audio into text in real-time or from a recording. It converts fragments of sound into text using the acoustic model and then uses the language model to create words and phrases. Speech to Text converts audio from a range of sources, including microphones, audio files, and Azure Blob storage.

The Speech to Text API can be used synchronously (real-time) or asynchronously (batch). There are two separate APIs: one for short audio (up to 60 seconds) that you can transcribe in real-time, and the other for batch transcription. The batch Speech to Text API can translate large volumes of speech audio recordings stored in Azure Blob Storage.

More than 85 languages and variants are supported.

You can see how Speech to Text works without an Azure subscription at https://azure.microsoft.com/services/cognitive-services/speech-to-text, as shown in Figure 4-14.

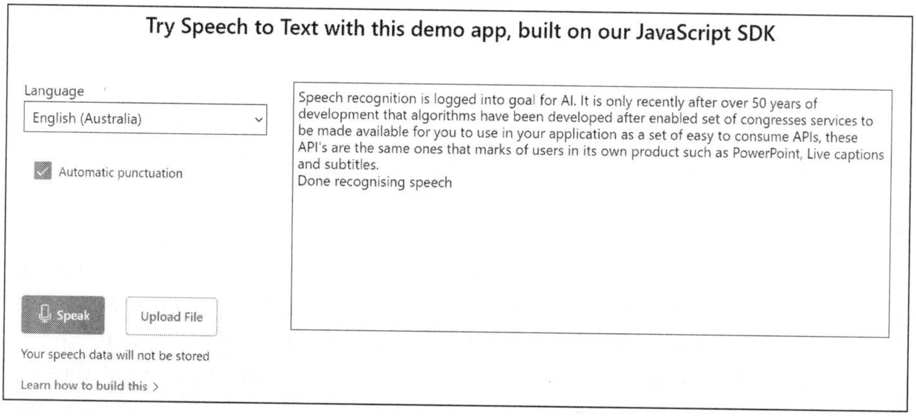

FIGURE 4-14 Speech to Text

In this example, the first paragraph from this section was read aloud using the computer's microphone. The speech was recognized and transcribed reasonably accurately but has a couple of errors. It could not differentiate between 15 and 50, and mis-transcribed Cognitive as "congresses." The Speech to Text service is typically faster and more accurate than a human being can achieve.

Speech to Text partitions the audio based on the speakers' voices to determine who said what. This allows you to obtain transcripts with automatic formatting and punctuation.

Text to Speech

Text to Speech is useful when you cannot look at a screen if you are controlling other equipment or are using a mobile device. Text to Speech generates, or synthesizes, text into spoken audio.

The Text to Speech API converts text into synthesized speech. You can choose from neutral voices, standard voices, or a custom voice. You can also create your own custom voice for use in speech synthesis. There are over 200 voices available, and the Text to Speech service supports over 60 languages and variants.

You can see how Text to Speech works without an Azure subscription at https://azure.microsoft.com/services/cognitive-services/text-to-speech, as shown in Figure 4-15.

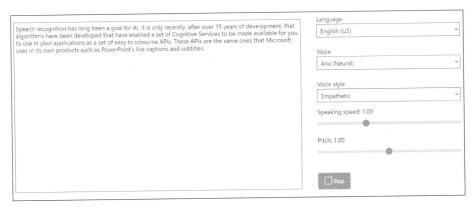

FIGURE 4-15 Text to Speech

In this example, the first paragraph from this section is synthesized into audio and played through the computer's speakers. The results are very impressive and very lifelike.

Speech Translation

You could achieve translation of speech yourself using a mixture of the Speech to Text, Translator, and Text to Speech services. The Speech Translation service simplifies this process for you. It first detects and transcribes speech into text; then it processes to make it easier for translation. The text is then fed to the text translation service to convert to the target language. Finally, the translated text is synthesized into audio.

Speech Translation converts audio into text and translates into another language in real-time or in batch. Speech Translation can translate audio into more than 60 languages. Speech Translation performs both speech-to-text and speech-to-speech translations.

You can see how Speech Translation works without an Azure subscription at https://azure.microsoft.com/services/cognitive-services/speech-translation, as shown in Figure 4-16.

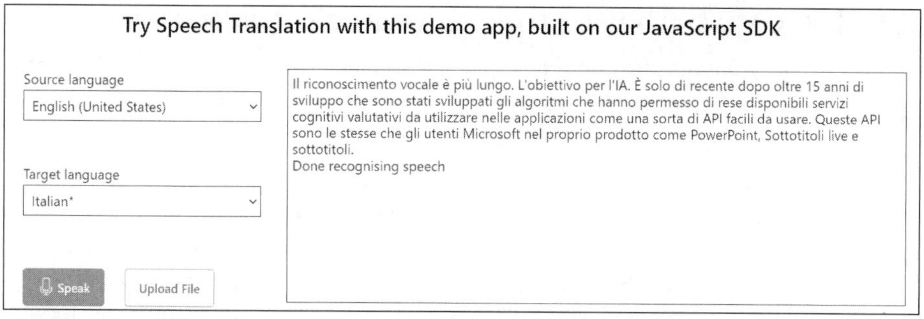

Try Speech Translation with this demo app, built on our JavaScript SDK

Source language

English (United States)

Target language

Italian*

Il riconoscimento vocale è più lungo. L'obiettivo per l'IA. È solo di recente dopo oltre 15 anni di sviluppo che sono stati sviluppati gli algoritmi che hanno permesso di rese disponibili servizi cognitivi valutativi da utilizzare nelle applicazioni come una sorta di API facili da usare. Queste API sono le stesse che gli utenti Microsoft nel proprio prodotto come PowerPoint, Sottotitoli live e sottotitoli.
Done recognising speech

Speak   Upload File

FIGURE 4-16 Speech Translation

In this example, the first paragraph from this section was read aloud using the computer's microphone. The speech was recognized and translated into the target language. However, it has not translated it correctly; the first half of the text has been split incorrectly into sentences and has several errors. The second half is reasonably well translated.

Speaker Recognition

Speaker Recognition identifies speakers from their voice characteristics in an audio clip. Speaker Recognition answers the question: "Who is speaking?"

To be identified, speakers must be enrolled using sample audio recordings of their voice. The Speaker Recognition service extracts the characteristics of the voice to form a profile. This profile is used to verify that the speaker is the same person (speaker verification) or to identify the speakers in a conversation (speaker diarization). Speaker diarization can be used to assist in creating transcripts of conversations.

Use cases for Speech

Mobile phone apps are a common use case for speech-related services. Many apps now use speech to text, text to speech, and speaker recognition. There are apps such as Microsoft Translator that work on your mobile and translate speech across two languages.

Personal Digital Assistants such as Cortana use the Speech service to take instructions and questions as audio through the microphone and respond with audio. You will find speech services in home automation.

My banking app allows me to use my voice to identify me. I had to enroll my voice in the app by saying the statement "My identity is secure because my voice is my passport, verify me" three times. I can now access my banking details by repeating the same phrase.

Telephony data that is generated through landlines and mobile phones is typically low quality, which creates challenges when converting speech into text. Recent improvements in the Speech service have significantly increased the accuracy of transcribing telephone call recordings.

Identify the capabilities of the Translator service

The Translator service translates text from one source language (from) into multiple other (to) languages. The Translator service allows you to specify multiple "to" languages, so you can simultaneously translate into multiple languages.

The Translator service uses Neural Machine Translation (NMT). NMT uses neural networks and deep learning to translate whole sentences. Statistical Machine Translation (SMT) technology uses statistical analysis to estimate the best possible translations for a word given in the context of a few neighboring words. Translator replaced SMT with NMT in 2016.

The Translator service can translate text in real-time or batch across 90 languages, variants, and dialects.

Create a Translator resource

Translator is a non-regional service, and you should create your resource in the Global region, unless your application requires a specific region.

The Translator service can be deployed in the Azure portal by searching for Translator when creating a new resource. You must select your region, select the resource group, provide a unique name, and select the pricing tier: Free F0 or tiers with volume discounts.

You can create a Translator resource using the CLI as follows:

```
az cognitiveservices account create --name <unique name> --resource-group <resource
group name> --kind TextTranslation --sku F0 --location Global
```

Use the Translator service

Translator is a modern JSON-based Web API. There are several operations that can be performed:

- **Language**   Returns the list of languages supported by the service.
- **Detect**   Identifies the language of the source text.
- **Translate**   Translation of text from one language into multiple languages.
- **Transliteration**   Translation of text from one language into another language and changing the script/character set.
- **BreakSentence**   Identifies the position of the sentences in the text.
- **Dictionary Lookup**   Provides alternative translations of a word or phrase.
- **Dictionary Example**   Provides examples of how a word or phrase is used.

The request URL for the translate operation is formulated as follows:

```
https://api.cognitive.microsofttranslator.com/translate?api-version=3.0&to<language
code>
```

The Translator service supports translation into language variants such as French and Canadian French. The Translator service allows you to specify a cultural variant when translating into a language. You append the cultural code to the language code—for example, fr-CA for Canadian French—to the URL request.

Following is the JSON returned for a paragraph at the beginning of this section translated from English (en) to Spanish (es):

```
[{detectedLanguage: {language: "en", score: 1.0},

translations: [{to: "es", text: "El servicio Traductor puede traducir simultáneamente
de un idioma a varios otros idiomas. El servicio Traductor traduce texto de un idioma a
otro idioma. El servicio Traductor le permite especificar varios idiomas, para que pueda
traducir simultáneamente a varios idiomas."}]}]
```

There are limits in the Translator API:

- Translate operation is limited to 10,000 characters, including spaces.
- Transliterate operation is limited to 5,000 characters.
- Detect operation is limited to 50,000 characters.
- Dictionary Lookup operation is limited to 1,000 characters.

Use cases for Translator

Earlier in this section, we gave an example of a mobile app that translates from one language into another. There are many such apps that make life easier for the traveler.

There are other use cases for translation support, such as translating speech and text in multi-country call centers.

You could create a multi-language website using Translator or build an app that supports multiple languages.

Microsoft PowerPoint provides real-time translation of presentation as subtitles. The Live Presentations feature allows audience members to see the presentation on their mobile device with subtitles generated from your speech translated into their language.

Chapter summary

In this chapter, you learned some of the general concepts related to Natural Language Processing. You learned about the features of Natural Language Processing, and you learned about the services in Azure Cognitive Services related to language and speech. Here are the key concepts from this chapter:

- Natural Language Processing is about extracting information and insights from both speech and text.
- NLP use statistical analysis and other processes to extract meaning from text.
- NLP uses a language model to understand the text.
- Key phrase extraction finds the main topics in the text.
- Named entity recognition identifies known entities (people, places, and things) in the text.
- Sentiment analysis classifies the emotion in the text as positive or negative.

- Speech recognition detects and interprets audio and converts it to text.

- Speech synthesis generates spoken audio from text.

- Translation converts text from one language into another language.

- The Text Analytics service is an Azure Cognitive Service that performs a series of Natural Language Processing operations on text, including detection of language, sentiment analysis, key phrase extraction, and named entity recognition.

- The Language Understanding service (LUIS) is an Azure Cognitive Service that analyzes user input to understand the meaning of the input text.

- LUIS extracts from the text what the user wants and what the user is talking about using intents, utterances, and entities.

- An intent is the action that the user wants to perform.

- An utterance is an example phrase that a user says. You need to supply sample utterances to train your model.

- Entities are the subjects or context for the intent.

- There are prebuilt entities for common objects, such as dates, places, and personal information (PII). You can add your own custom entities for your business domain.

- Features provide hints for LUIS to use to find intent and entities.

- A LUIS app requires both an authoring resource and a prediction resource to be provisioned in Azure.

- Speech to Text transcribes audio into text in real-time or from audio files.

- Speech to Text can transcribe large quantities of audio recordings stored in Azure Blob Storage.

- Text to Speech synthesizes text into spoken audio.

- You can create a custom voice for conversion of text into synthesized speech.

- Speech Translation converts audio into text and translates into another language in real-time.

- Speaker Recognition identifies enrolled people from their voices in an audio clip.

- Translator translates text in real-time or in batch.

- Translator supports translation into many languages and variants.

> **NEED MORE REVIEW?** **HANDS-ON LABS**
>
> For more hands-on experience with Natural Language Processing, complete labs 7 to 10 at https://github.com/MicrosoftLearning/mslearn-ai900.

Thought experiment

Let's apply what you have learned in this chapter. In this thought experiment, demonstrate your skills and knowledge of the topics covered in this chapter. You can find the answers in the section that follows.

You work for Litware, Inc., a company with several brands that supplies business to business services across the world. Litware is interested in analyzing the large amount of text involved in their business using AI.

Litware wants to evaluate how Cognitive Services can improve their internal document categorization.

Litware wants to create a single support desk to handle their worldwide customer base. This central desk will provide consistent responses to customers no matter their location or language.

Litware needs to understand how customers will respond to this move to a single support desk. Customers are sent a questionnaire to ask them about this move. The questionnaire has a series of questions and includes a space for the customer to write their thoughts on this move. Customers can also make a request as part of the questionnaire for more information or for someone to contact them.

As part of this planned move, Litware monitors social media for mentions about these proposed changes and records telephone calls into the existing support desks.

Answer the following questions:

1. Which workload is used to evaluate how the customer feels about the move to a central support desk?
2. Which workload is used to discover the topics mentioned by customers in the questionnaire?
3. Named entity recognition extracts the intent and action from the request in the questionnaire. Is this correct?
4. Which workload is used to monitor social media for negative mentions of Litware's brands?
5. Which workload is used to transcribe telephone calls into the support desk?
6. Which Cognitive Service would you use to mine customer perceptions of Litware's products and services?
7. What examples of how users phrase their requests do you need to provide to the LUIS app?
8. For what information do you need to use a published Language Understanding model to find the meaning in a text statement?
9. Which service do you use to translate the large volumes of telephone calls?
10. Do you have to use a standard voice, or can you create a custom voice for text to speech?

Thought experiment answers

This section contains the solutions to the thought experiment. Each answer explains why the answer choice is correct.

1. The emotion expressed in text is an example of the sentiment analysis workload. Sentiment analysis evaluates a piece of text and determines if the text has a positive or negative feeling/emotion.

2. The topics, or main talking points, contained in text is an example of the key phrase extraction workload. Key phrase extraction evaluates the text and identifies the key talking points in the text.

3. No, the intent and actions expressed in text are an example of language understanding and not named entity recognition. Language understanding extracts the overall meaning from the text.

4. Analyzing social media for a brand is an example of where you would use sentiment analysis to determine the positive and negative mentions of a brand.

5. Transcription of a recording into text is an example of speech recognition. Speech recognition can convert audio into text.

6. Mining customer opinions can be performed by Text Analytics using the sentiment analysis operation. Sentiment analysis explores customers' perceptions of products or services.

7. You need to add sample utterances to train the LUIS model.

8. To use a Language Understanding (LUIS) model to find the intent of a text statement, you need the ID of the LUIS app and the endpoint and key for the prediction resource.

9. The Speech to Text API can be used synchronously (real-time) or asynchronously (batch). Batch Speech to Text can translate large volumes of speech audio recordings stored in Azure Blob Storage.

10. You can choose from neutral voices, standard voices, or a custom voice. The Text to Speech API can create custom voices.

Describe features of conversational AI workloads on Azure

We now use multiple communications channels such as email, webchat, telephone, chat, and multiple social media platforms—for example, Slack, Teams, and Facebook. Organizations need to be able to be contactable by their customers over these multiple channels, and they need to respond consistently in the same manner no matter which channel a customer decides to use.

Customers are becoming more demanding. They require 24x7 responses, responses that are tailored to their behaviors and characteristics, and responses to more and more complex requests.

Conversational AI is the use of AI-powered agents, known as bots, to respond to human questions and requests in an intelligent way. Organizations use bots to provide the first line of response to customers, handling common inquiries across multiple channels. Bots instigate a conversational dialog with the human, whether that is over the web or another channel such as the SMS text service.

This chapter explains the conversational AI capabilities provided by Microsoft Azure. First, the concepts involved will be outlined with use cases, followed by how to use the Azure services involved.

Skills covered in this chapter:

- Skill 5.1: Identify common use cases for conversational AI
- Skill 5.2: Identify Azure services for conversational AI

Skill 5.1: Identify common use cases for conversational AI

When humans interact with a computer application using text and speech, the human should not be expected to imitate the application's internal instructions; this only causes irritation and ultimately leads the human to abandon using the app. A computer application must be able to handle language provided in a natural way and be able to react accordingly to the meaning that the human has expressed. Conversational AI bridges the gap between human and computer language; it allows humans and computer applications to work together in a natural way.

Conversational AI allows computers to recognize human language, interpret different languages, understand what is being said, and respond in a manner that mimics a human conversation.

You probably have experienced webchat bots yourself, but conversational AI is more than building webchat bots, although this is one of the main use cases for conversational AI.

Figure 5-1 shows how a webchat bot works. A human asks the question, "How can I book an exam?"

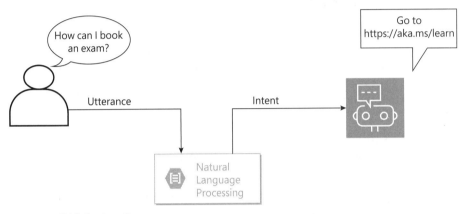

FIGURE 5-1 Webchat bot diagram

This question is processed using Natural Language Processing (NLP) that was described in the previous chapter. NLP uses a language model to extract the meaning from the question and pass it to the bot as an intent that the bot can understand. The bot can formulate a response by integrating to other systems or by using a database.

A good definition of conversational AI is a natural dialog between an AI agent and a human. This dialog can occur over many different communication channels, such as web, social media, email, or voice.

The Microsoft Azure AI Fundamentals certification includes the capabilities and features of conversational AI and how conversational AI can be applied in solutions requiring dialogs with users. This requires you to understand the use cases for conversational AI.

This skill covers how to:
- Identify features and uses for webchat bots
- Identify common characteristics of conversational AI solutions

Identify features and uses for webchat bots

A *webchat* is an online conversation between a user and a human advisor. Webchat requires a team of human agents to handle the user requests. A *webchat bot* is an online application that helps users solve a problem without a human agent.

The most common use for bots is on websites where the bot provides automated chat to users browsing a website or a web-based platform.

A webchat bot has a text input box for the user to type their question. On some webchat bots, you may also see a microphone icon that enables speech input. Figure 5-2 shows a screenshot of a webchat bot.

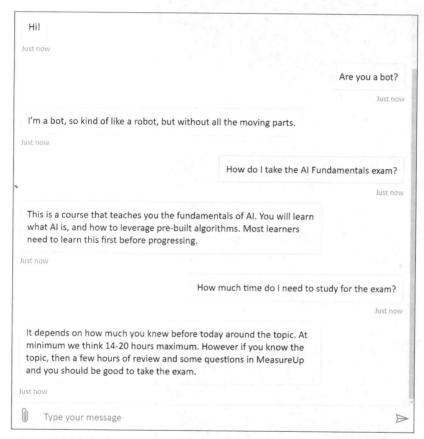

FIGURE 5-2 Webchat bot example

Webchat bots provide automated responses to customers. Webchat bots manage the conversation using a combination of natural language and predefined responses to guide the customer to a resolution.

Use cases for webchat bots

A popular use for webchat bots is in customer support scenarios. For example, if you visit the HP support site https://support.hp.com/, a webchat bot will assist you with troubleshooting, warranty, and repairs.

Webchat bots are often used to provide answers to frequently asked questions (FAQs). Figure 5-3 shows a screenshot of a webchat bot that provides FAQs inside Facebook Messenger.

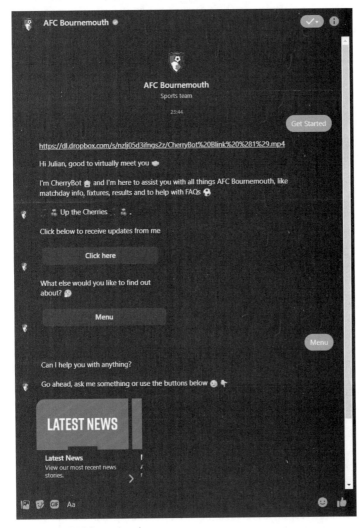

FIGURE 5-3 FAQ bot example

This bot is an FAQ bot for a professional soccer team in the United Kingdom, AFC Bournemouth, whose nickname is the Cherries. The bot is named CherryBot. CherryBot answers common questions about the club and attending games.

Another common use case for webchat bots is in the online ordering process or for travel reservation and booking. For example, the Seattle Ballooning website https://seattleballooning.com/experience/ allows you to book your ballooning experience via a chatbot. Figure 5-4 shows a screenshot of this bot.

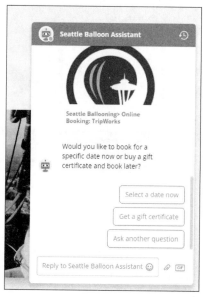

FIGURE 5-4 Online ordering bot example

This bot asks a series of questions that allows customers to tailor their experience and to choose what they want to book.

You will find webchat bots on ecommerce sites. There are even bots that help you decide which clothes to purchase.

A more recent use case for webchat bots has been in healthcare to triage people based on their symptoms. For example, the CDC has a Coronavirus Self-Checker bot on their website: https://www.cdc.gov/coronavirus/2019-ncov/symptoms-testing/coronavirus-self-checker.html. This bot was built using the Azure services described in this chapter.

Identify common characteristics of conversational AI solutions

There is more to conversational AI than webchat. You will find conversational AI in personal digital assistants, such as Cortana and Siri. *Personal digital assistants*, also known as *virtual assistants*, are apps built into your phone, watch, and other devices that respond to text and spoken language and act on your behalf.

Interactive Voice Response (IVR) on telephone systems are another area where you might find conversational AI being used.

A virtual assistant responds to a command by taking action—for example, creating a booking for you in your calendar.

Cortana is an example of a personal digital assistant, although it refers to itself as a personal productivity assistant. Figure 5-5 shows a screenshot of Cortana answering a question.

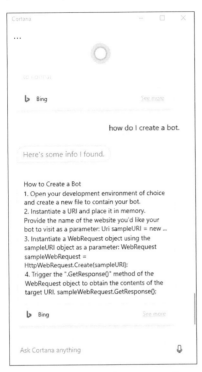

FIGURE 5-5 Cortana assistant answering a question

Cortana responds both with text and speech utilizing the Speech services discussed in the previous chapter. Cortana can:

- Manage your calendar
- Join a meeting in Microsoft Teams
- Set reminders
- Find information on the web
- Open apps on your computer

Windows 10 includes the Microsoft Virtual Assistant that you can start by pressing the Start key and typing Get Help. Figure 5-6 shows a screenshot of the Microsoft Virtual Assistant app.

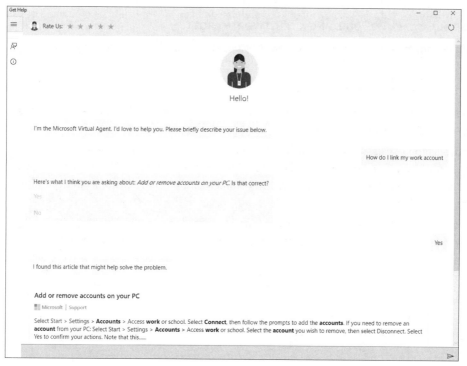

FIGURE 5-6 Microsoft Virtual Assistant app

The Microsoft Virtual Assistant responds to questions with links to Microsoft support pages and offers to escalate to a human agent. It is not a personal digital assistant, as defined previously, because it does not perform actions on your behalf.

Responsible AI for conversational AI

It is important that you remember the principles for Responsible AI when building solutions with conversational AI. The Transparency principle is one of the principles that particularly applies to bots.

> **NOTE RESPONSIBLE AI**
>
> The Transparency principle for Responsible AI was discussed in Chapter 1 and should be considered when building bots and using conversational AI.

A user should always know they are interacting with a bot. When a bot conversation is started, the bot should clearly state that it is a bot. The bot should state its purpose and limitation—for instance, by listing the scope of what the bot can answer or do. A bot should enable the user to escalate or transfer to a human.

Bots work well when they are limited solely to their purpose and do not try to be too generic.

Use cases for conversational AI

You have seen in this section several examples for conversational AI with personal digital assistants, such as Siri, Cortana, and Alexa.

Conversational AI can be added into applications to increase the user experience. For example, an insurance company might create an app for their customers. The app can act as a virtual advisor and make personalized policy recommendations to the customer in a question-and-answer dialog.

A conversational AI health app can answer queries related to a chronic health condition. It can provide guidance to the patient about any questions they might have and provide access to information. You might even use an app to detect a stroke from changes in the voice patterns of the patient.

The Microsoft Azure Health Bot (https://aka.ms/healthbot) is a bot that you can deploy from within Azure. The bot contains a symptom checker, medical content from industry sources, and a language model trained to understand medical terminology.

EXAM TIP

You need to be able to identify the use cases for conversational AI solutions or where applications that leverage conversational AI can be used to meet the scenario described.

Skill 5.2: Identify Azure services for conversational AI

The Azure Bot Framework provides tools and services to build enterprise-grade conversational AI apps from simple Q&A bots to fully fledged virtual assistants. The Azure Bot Framework allows you to natively integrate with Azure Cognitive Services such as LUIS, Text Analytics, and Speech to enable your bot to have meaningful conversations with users. You can also leverage other Cognitive Services such as Computer Vision and Azure Cognitive Search to increase the user experience for your app.

The Azure Bot Framework contains Software Development Kits (SDKs) for .NET, Python, and JavaScript so you can build bots with the programming languages you are familiar with. The Azure Bot Framework contains various templates and tools to enable you to create, test, and deploy bots easily.

The Microsoft Azure AI Fundamentals certification requires you to understand the Azure AI services for conversational AI and how to differentiate between them.

This skill covers how to:

- Identify capabilities of the QnA Maker service
- Identify capabilities of the Azure Bot Service

Identify capabilities of the QnA Maker service

QnA Maker is a service that creates a searchable knowledge base from existing documents and websites. This knowledge base contains built-in Natural Language Processing. The QnA Maker knowledge base can then be used in bots and other applications to respond to FAQ-type questions.

QnA Maker is part of the language services in Azure Cognitive Services but is typically used when creating conversational AI solutions. QnA Maker does not provide a bot itself, but you can easily generate a bot from your QnA Maker knowledge base in a few minutes without writing any code.

A portal is provided where you can create QnA Maker knowledge bases. A knowledge base consists of question-and-answer pairs. You can create the questions and answers in a number of different ways:

- Extraction from existing documents
- Extraction from webpages
- Manual input

You will use a mixture of these techniques to build your knowledge base, starting with existing sources and adding other questions, alternative phrasing, and answers manually.

EXAM TIP

As the easiest way of creating a bot without code, you can expect to be asked questions about the capabilities of QnA Maker and the process you undertake to build a bot powered by a QnA Maker knowledge base.

QnA Maker resource

To use QnA Maker, you must first create a QnA Maker resource in Azure.

To create a resource for QnA Maker in the Azure portal, search for QnA and pick the service titled QnA Maker, as shown in Figure 5-7.

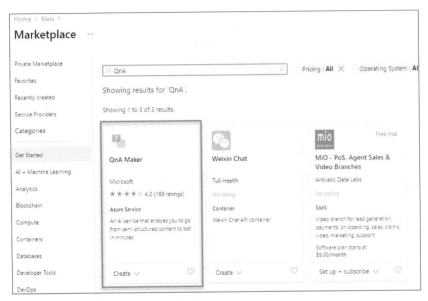

FIGURE 5-7 QnA Maker in Azure Marketplace

Clicking on Create will show the description for the service, as shown in Figure 5-8.

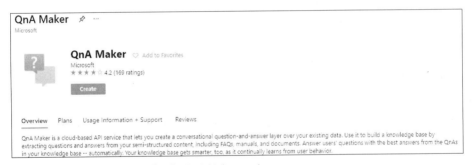

FIGURE 5-8 Service description for the QnA Maker service

After clicking on the Create button, the Create QnA Maker pane opens, as shown in Figure 5-9.

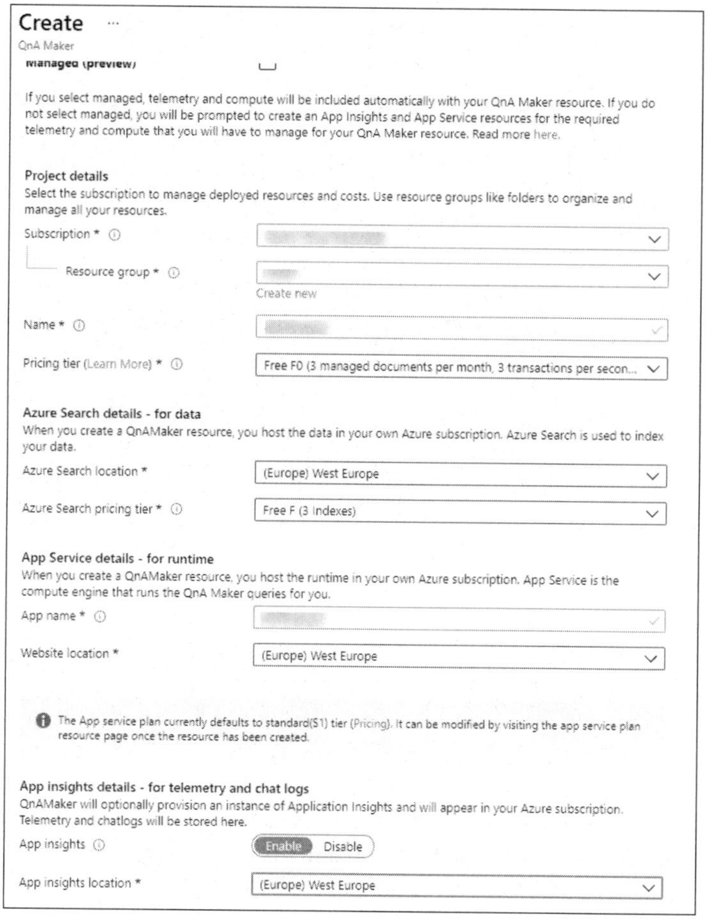

FIGURE 5-9 Creating QnA Maker resources

You will need to select your subscription and resource group. You will then need to create a unique name for the service. This name will be the domain name for your endpoints and so must be unique worldwide. There are four resources to create: QnA Maker, Azure Search, App Service, and App Insights. For each of these, you need to select the region and pricing tier. Free tiers are available.

Clicking on Review + Create will validate the options. You then click on Create to create the resources.

You can create the QnA Maker resources using the CLI as follows:

```
az cognitiveservices account create --name <unique name for authoring> --resource-
group <resource group name> --kind LUIS.Authoring --sku F0 --location <region> --api-
properties qnaRuntimeEndpoint=<URL Endpoint for App Service>
```

Once your resources have been created, you will need to obtain the REST API URL and the key to access the resources. To view the endpoint and keys in the Azure portal, navigate to the resource and click on Keys and Endpoint, as shown in Figure 5-10.

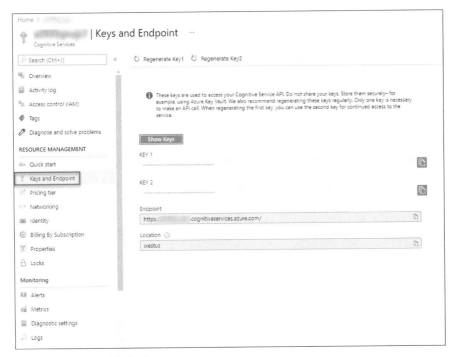

FIGURE 5-10 Keys and Endpoint

QnA Maker portal

QnA Maker uses a web portal (https://www.qnamaker.ai) where you can create your knowledge base, add key value pairs, train the model, and finally publish the knowledge base.

The process for creating a knowledge base is as follows:

1. Name the knowledge base.
2. Populate the knowledge base from files and website URLs.
3. Create the knowledge base.
4. Train the knowledge base.
5. Test the knowledge base.
6. Publish the knowledge base to an endpoint.

Once you have created your QnA Maker resources, you can open the QnA Maker web portal (https://www.qnamaker.ai) in a browser. After clicking Create a knowledge base, you will be presented with five steps. The first step is to create a QnA Maker resource. This will open the Azure portal, as shown in Figure 5-9. Because you have already created a QnA Maker resource, you can skip this step and continue to Step 2 to select your subscription and your QnA Maker resource, as shown in Figure 5-11.

Step 3 is to name your knowledge base.

Step 4 is to populate the knowledge base with existing files and links to webpages, as shown in Figure 5-12.

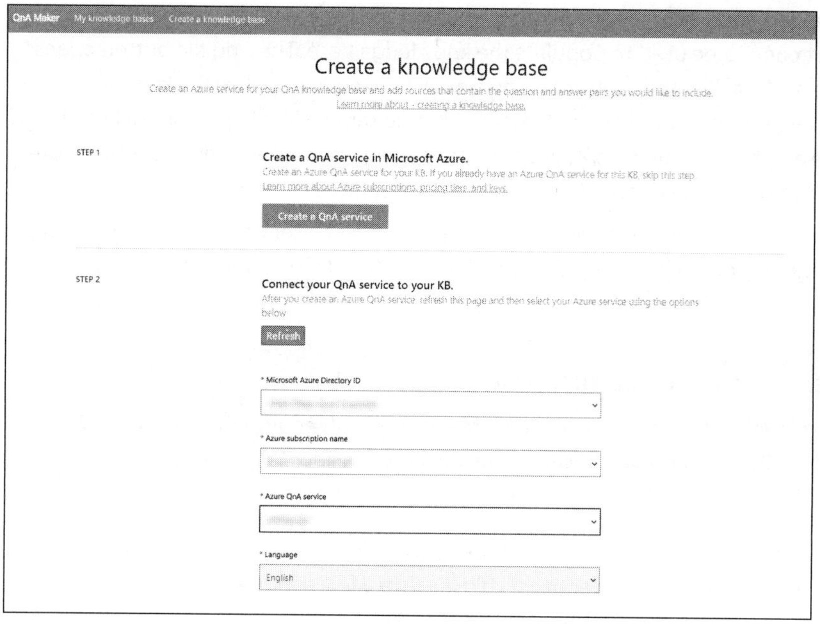

FIGURE 5-11 Selecting the QnA Maker resource

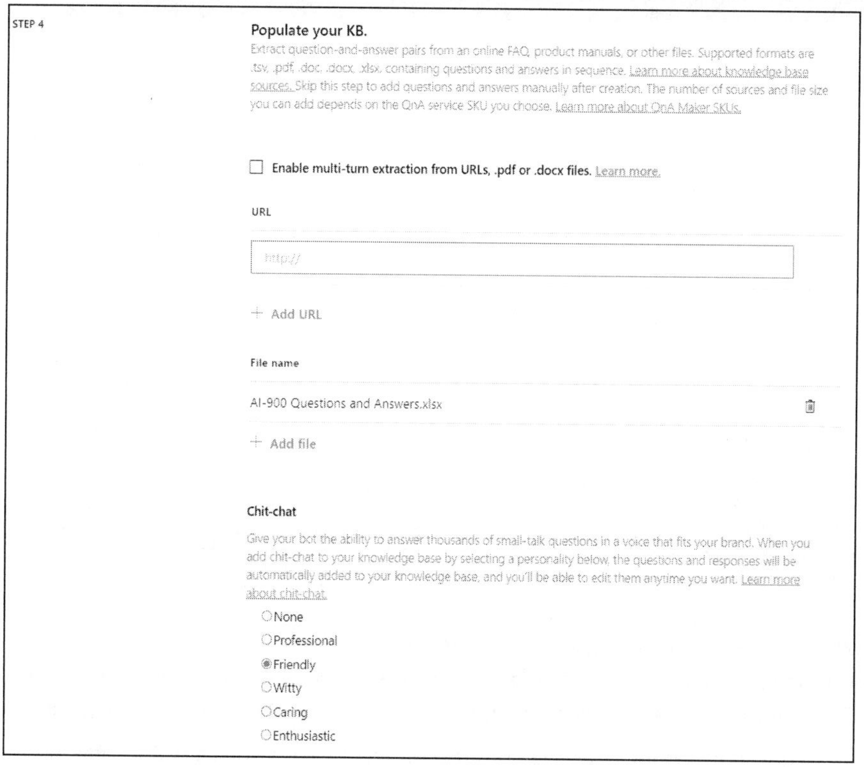

FIGURE 5-12 Populate your KB

There is a field to enter a URL to the existing webpage. Clicking on Add URL will enable the contents of that page to be used to populate the knowledge base. The Add file button opens Explorer to select a local file. The contents of the file will be used to populate the knowledge base. You can have a mixture of URLs and files. You can find sample files to populate a knowledge base on GitHub at https://github.com/Azure-Samples/cognitive-services-sample-data-files/tree/master/qna-maker/data-source-formats.

Step 4 allows you to define the personality of the responses generated from the knowledge base by selecting the chit-chat setting. Chit-chat files are stored in Tab Separated Value (TSV) format.

> **NOTE** **POPULATING THE KNOWLEDGE BASE**
>
> You can only add files and URLs from public sources that do not require authentication, with the exception of files in SharePoint document folders. You can add Word documents, Excel worksheets, PDF files, and text files in Tab Separated Value (TSV) format.

The final step is to create your knowledge base. QnA Maker will analyze the sources you added to extract question-and-answer pairs. This will take a few minutes, and when complete, you can view the knowledge base, as shown in Figure 5-13.

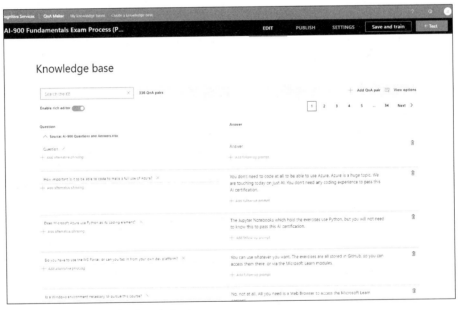

FIGURE 5-13 The QnA Maker knowledge base

The knowledge base consists of question-and-answer pairs. You can edit the knowledge base manually and add further question-and-answer pairs or add alternative phrasing for the questions. The editorial source indicates the QnA pair was added in the QnA portal manually.

Sometimes a question cannot be answered with a single response; you can add follow-up prompts, which will be listed as choices for the user to pick from. For example, you can respond to the question "How do I create a Cognitive Services resource" with two options: Single service or Multiple service.

Once you have completed editing the knowledge base, you can save and train the knowledge base. This should only take a few minutes.

You can test the knowledge base directly in the portal shown in Figure 5-14.

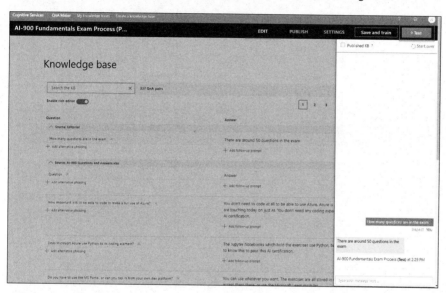

FIGURE 5-14 Testing the QnA Maker knowledge base

You can now publish the knowledge base. This creates an endpoint that can be used by bots and other applications.

After publishing your knowledge base, QnA Maker gives you the option to create a bot, as shown in Figure 5-15.

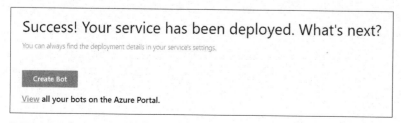

FIGURE 5-15 Create a QnA Maker bot

Clicking on the Create Bot button opens the Azure portal, as shown in Figure 5-16.

FIGURE 5-16 Create a QnA Maker bot

You need to create a unique name for the bot. This name will be the domain name for the web app used by the bot and so must be unique worldwide. You will need to select your subscription, resource group, region, and pricing tier. A Free tier is available. After you click on Create, the code for your bot will be generated, and you can select from C# or Node.js. This code can be downloaded and customized. Clicking on Create will automatically generate and deploy the bot using the Azure Bot Service.

You can test the bot in the Azure Portal from within the bot's resource page. The bot shown at the beginning of the chapter in Figure 5-2 is a bot generated from a QnA Maker knowledge base.

Now that you have created a bot, let's have a look in more detail at the Azure Bot Service.

Identify capabilities of the Azure Bot Service

The Azure Bot Service is part of the Azure Bot Framework, a series of SDKs and tools that allow developers to create and deploy custom bots and virtual assistants using code. The Azure Bot Service is a managed service for developing bots.

A bot communicates by receiving messages and sending responses using an Azure Web App to handle the communications. Bots are like web applications; they take requests and return responses. A bot can perform operations like other applications; they can access databases, call APIs to other services, read files, and perform calculations.

The process of receiving a message and sending a response back to the user is known as a "turn." Think how conversations between humans work; each person speaks one at a time—i.e., in turn. Bots operate the same way, responding to user input in turn.

The Bot Service does not understand natural language and cannot handle when a user does not use the terms that the code in the bot expects. It is, however, straightforward for a developer to connect an Azure Bot Service bot with a LUIS app to add language understanding to a bot and for a bot to use a knowledge base created in QnA Maker.

An advantage of the Azure Bot Service is that once developers have built the bot, you can deploy the bot to one or more channels, such as Facebook or Slack, without having to change the bot's code. The Bot Service takes care of the communication between these services and your bots. The Bot Service adapts the messages your bot generates to the format of the service it is connected to.

Bot Framework SDK

The Bot Framework SDK is required to develop bots using code. There are SDKs for C#, JavaScript, and Python.

The Bot Framework SDK makes it straightforward for developers to add turns to the bot to handle the different messages sent by users and to create a conversational flow. The developer can focus on adding the code for the intents, actions, and entities rather than having to write code for the communications over different channels.

The Bot Framework SDK contains several dialogs that simplify coding, such as prompting for user input, and adaptive cards that display a list of actions a user can take.

Bot Service templates

The Bot Service includes templates to help developers get started with building bots. If you create a bot in the Azure Portal, you can select either the Echo bot template that just returns the user input, or the Basic bot template that includes LUIS. These templates are available in C# and Node.js, as shown in Figure 5-17.

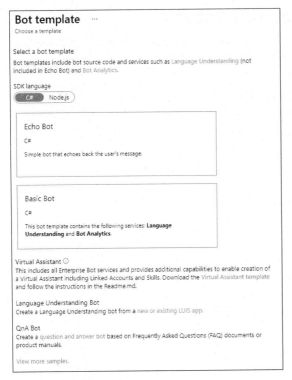

FIGURE 5-17 Bot templates

On this pane, there is a link to the Visual Studio extension for creating a bot using the Virtual Assistant template, a link to the instructions to create a bot that integrates with LUIS, and a link to the instructions to create a bot from a QnA Maker knowledge base.

> **NOTE BOT TEMPLATES**
>
> There are further bot templates available on GitHub at https://github.com/microsoft/BotBuilder-Samples.

Integrating bots with LUIS and QnA Maker

Understanding language is a key requirement for bots, and the Azure Bot Service makes it straightforward to use a LUIS app with an Azure Bot Service bot. A developer can add LUIS to a bot when they create the bot or add LUIS later. A developer will use the Dispatch tool to route messages from the bot to LUIS.

You have already seen that you can generate a bot from a QnA Maker knowledge base. A developer can integrate a bot they have built with any QnA Maker knowledge base. A developer will use the Dispatch tool to route messages from the bot to QnA Maker. The code within the bot can choose which has the best response for the user.

Language Understanding (LUIS) and QnA Maker are often both used in a bot. They deal with different types of requests; LUIS determines the intent of a user's request, while QnA Maker determines the answer to a user's request.

When a user sends a message to a bot, it can pass the request to both QnA Maker and LUIS. QnA Maker and LUIS will both respond back to the bot with a confidence score, and the bot can then decide which response to send back to the user.

If the request is answered from the QnA Maker knowledge base with high confidence, then that may be the best response to the customer. If the QnA Maker knowledge base does not have a response, or has a response with low confidence, and LUIS returns a response with high confidence, then the bot can use the LUIS intent and entity to formulate the response to the user.

Bot Framework Emulator

When developing bots, a developer can test their bot inside of the Azure Portal. However, this only allows for simple testing and requires the developer to publish the bot to Azure after each change.

A better option is to use the Azure Bot Framework Emulator. The Bot Framework Emulator is a Windows desktop application that allows developers to test and debug bots on their local computer.

Composer

The Bot Framework Composer is a tool to build bots. Bot Composer supports both LUIS and QnA Maker.

The Bot Framework Composer uses a visual user interface to create the conversational flow and generate responses. Composer is a recent addition to Azure Bot Services and is the subject of ongoing development to add further features. Microsoft intends for Composer to be the primary tool for developing bots.

The Bot Framework Composer is open source and is multi-platform with support for Windows, Linux, and MacOS. You can find Bot Composer on GitHub at https://github.com/microsoft/BotFramework-Composer.

Channels

The Azure Bot Framework separates the logic of the bot from the communication with different services. When you create a bot, the bot is only available for use embedded on websites with the Web Chat channel. You can add channels to your bot to make the bot available on other platforms and services.

One of the major benefits of the Azure Bot Service is that you develop your bot once and connect to multiple channels without needing to change the code for each channel to handle the specific requirements and formats of that channel. The Azure Bot Service takes care of those requirements and converting the formats.

The following channels are available for connection to bots:

- Alexa
- Direct Line
- Direct Line Speech
- Email
- Facebook
- GroupMe
- Kik
- Line
- Microsoft Teams
- Skype
- Slack
- Telegram
- Telephone
- Twilio (SMS)
- Web Chat

Bot Lifecycle

The process for developing and deploying a bot is as follows:

- **Plan** Decide on the goal for your bot, and decide if your bot requires LUIS, Speech, or QnA Maker support. This is also a good time to reflect on the principles of Responsible AI and how they will be applied to your bot.
- **Build** Coding of the bot.
- **Test** Testing of bots is very important to make sure the bot is behaving as expected.
- **Publish** Once testing is complete, the developer can publish the bot to Azure.
- **Connect to Channels** Connect the bot to the channels where you want your bot to be used from.
- **Evaluate** Bots typically are never finished. There are always changes to the business domain that the bot is servicing, and that might mean the bot is not as effective as it once was. You need to monitor how the bot is performing.

We will now walk you through creating a bot using the Azure Bot Service. First, you need an Azure Bot Service resource.

To create an Azure Bot resource in the Azure portal, search for Bot and pick the service titled Web App Bot, as shown in Figure 5-18.

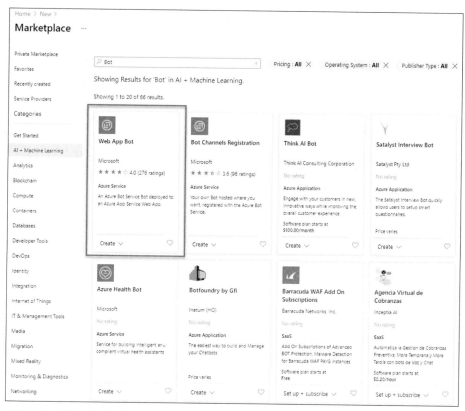

FIGURE 5-18 Web App Bot in Azure Marketplace

Clicking on Create will show the description for the service, as shown in Figure 5-19.

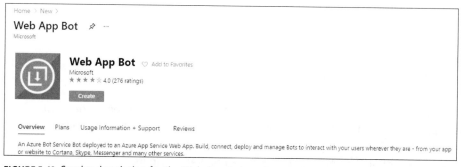

FIGURE 5-19 Service description for the Web App Bot service

After clicking on the Create button, the Create Web App Bot pane opens, as shown in Figure 5-20.

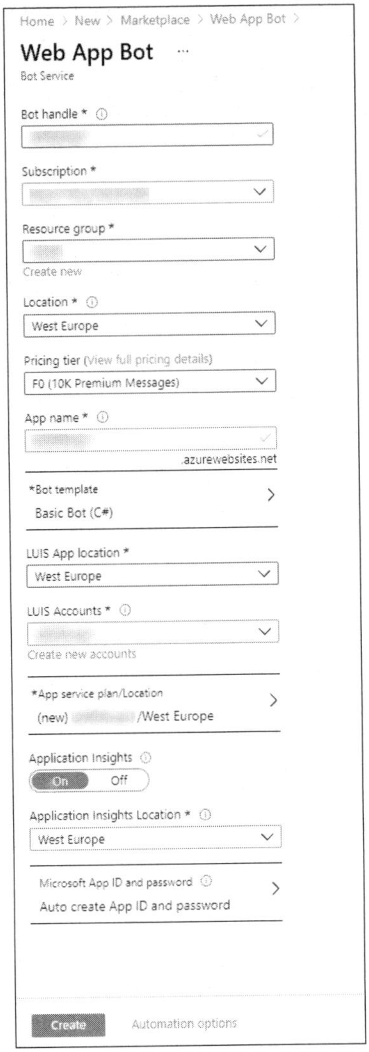

FIGURE 5-20 Creating Web App Bot resources

You need to create a unique name for the bot. This name will be the domain name for the web app used by the bot and so must be unique worldwide. You will need to select your subscription, resource group, region, and pricing tier. A Free tier is available. There are four resources to create: Bot, Web App, App Service Plan, and App Insights.

You can select the template from which you create your bot. You can select from C# or Node.js templates. If you choose the Basic bot that includes LUIS, you will need to specify the LUIS app to use. Clicking on Create will automatically generate and deploy the bot using the Azure Bot Service.

The App Service plan will default to using the S1 tier. This can be changed after you have created the bot. Alternatively, create the App Service plan prior to creating the bot with your chosen tier and select when creating a bot.

After creating your bot, you can see the resources created in your resource group, as shown in Figure 5-21.

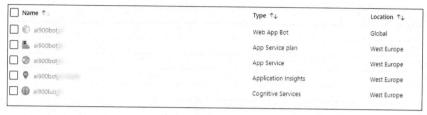

FIGURE 5-21 Web App Bot resources

You can create a Web App Bot resource using CLI. You must first register an app in Azure AD and then use the CLI command, as follows:

```
az bot create --name <bot handle> --resource-group <resource group name> --kind webapp
-appid <Azure AD App ID>
```

Once your resources have been created, you should open the Web App Bot resource and navigate to the overview pane, as shown in Figure 5-22.

FIGURE 5-22 Bot overview

Clicking on Download bot source code generates a ZIP file containing the source code for your bot. You can edit this source code with Visual Studio Code to add functionality and other processing, and then publish your changes back to the Bot Service.

> **NOTE BOT SOURCE CODE**
>
> **Customizing the source code for a bot is beyond the scope of AI Fundamentals.**

Clicking the Test in Web Chat opens the test pane for the bot, as shown in Figure 5-23.

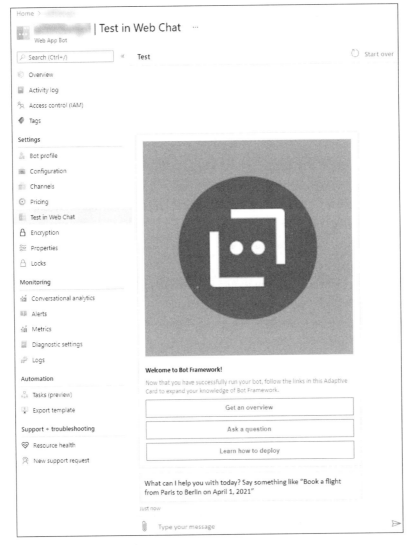

FIGURE 5-23 Test in Web Chat

You can test out your bot in this pane prior to deploying your bot.

Clicking on Connect to channels shows the currently enabled channels and allows you to deploy your bot to other channels, as shown in Figure 5-24.

FIGURE 5-24 Bot channels

Chapter summary

In this chapter, you learned some of the general concepts related to conversational AI. You learned about the features of conversational AI, and you learned about the services in Azure related to building bots. Here are the key concepts from this chapter:

- Conversational AI is a natural dialog between an AI agent and a human.
- Conversational AI allows computers to understand what is being said and respond in a manner that mimics a human conversation.
- A webchat bot is an online application that helps users solve a problem without a human agent.
- Webchat bots manage the conversation using a combination of natural language and predefined responses to guide the customer to a resolution.
- Webchat bots can use both text and speech.
- Webchat bots are one of the main use cases for conversational AI.
- Conversational AI is more than webchat; it includes personal digital assistants.
- A virtual assistant responds to a command by taking action.
- Virtual assistants use Speech-to-Text and Text-to-Speech services.
- Transparency is one of the principles of Responsible AI that applies to bots.
- The Azure Bot Framework provides tools and services to build enterprise-grade conversational AI apps.
- QnA Maker is a Cognitive service that creates a searchable knowledge base from existing documents and websites.

- QnA Maker can only access files and websites that are publicly available.

- QnA Maker extracts question-and-answer pairs from documents and websites.

- The personality of the responses from QnA Maker is defined by the chit-chat setting.

- QnA Maker knowledge bases must be trained and then published.

- A bot can be created from a QnA Maker knowledge base.

- There are Azure Bot Framework SDKs for .NET, JavaScript, and Python.

- The Azure Bot Service provides templates to accelerate the creation of bots.

- The Azure Bot Service can use LUIS to enable bots to understand human natural language and extract intents and entities.

- The Azure Bot Service bots can use QnA Maker knowledge bases to answer queries.

- The Azure Bot Framework separates the logic of the bot from the communication with different platforms.

- An Azure Service bot is enabled for the Web Chat channel by default.

- An Azure Service bot can be easily connected to other channels.

> **NEED MORE REVIEW?** **HANDS-ON LABS**
>
> For more hands-on experience with Natural Language Processing, complete lab 11 at https://github.com/MicrosoftLearning/mslearn-ai900.

Thought experiment

Let's apply what you have learned in this chapter. In this thought experiment, demonstrate your skills and knowledge of the topics covered in this chapter. You can find the answers in the section that follows.

You work for Tailspin Toys, a manufacturer of toys crafted from wood. Tailspin Toys are concerned with customer experience and want to implement an Omni-Channel customer support with an automated first-line solution.

Tailspin Toys plans to launch a new line of products that teaches children the basics of logic using moveable wooden tags to represent logic gates and wooden gears to demonstrate how data is processed. These educational toys will contain electrical contacts and sensors that will capture the positions of the wooden components. As part of this launch, an app for mobile phones is planned that can take pictures of the arrangement of the components and confirm if they are correct, showing videos if wrong, and reading out instructions to the customer. The app needs to use speech input. Users can request the bot to upload their pictures to a community board where customers can share their progress and experiences.

The existing support system relies on customer support agents accessing a variety of documents, databases, and applications, including the following:

- PDF files
- Excel spreadsheets

- An SQL database
- Various SharePoint lists
- Word documents held on SharePoint

Answer the following questions:

1. Publishing support questions and answers to frequently asked questions (FAQs) that can be accessed through a website or an app is an example of which workload?

2. Which requirement can be met by using a webchat bot?

3. What sort of workload shares the customers' photos?

4. Which sources could you use to populate a QnA Maker knowledge base?

5. Which Azure resources are created when a new QnA Marker service is created?

6. Which file format do you use for uploading a chit-chat personality to a QnA Maker knowledge base?

7. Which tool do you use to debug a bot built with the Azure Bot Framework?

8. What do you add to a bot to make it available on other platforms?

9. Which languages can you build bots in?

Thought experiment answers

This section contains the solutions to the thought experiment. Each answer explains why the answer choice is correct.

1. Webchat bots are conversational AI agents that can use Natural Language Processing to understand questions and find the most appropriate answer from a knowledge base.

2. Providing an automated first-line response to customers over multiple channels is the most common experience users will have with webchat bots.

3. A personal digital assistant acts on a user's behalf to perform actions such as uploading photos to the community board.

4. You can upload PDF, Excel, and Word documents into the QnA Maker portal. You cannot use the SQL database. You cannot use any URL that ends in .ASPX, such as SharePoint lists.

5. QnA Maker service creates an App Service, a Web App, Azure Search, and an Azure Cognitive Search resource.

6. Chit-chat files use the Tab Separated Value (TSV) format.

7. The Bot Framework Emulator is a desktop application that allows developers to test and debug bots on their local computer.

8. You add a channel to a bot to make the bot available on other platforms.

9. You can build a bot in several languages. There are SDKs for .NET, JavaScript, Python, and Java. You can also use the Bot Framework REST APIs.

Index

A

B

C

Plug into learning at

MicrosoftPressStore.com

The Microsoft Press Store by Pearson offers:

- Free U.S. shipping

- Buy an eBook, get three formats – Includes PDF, EPUB, and MOBI to use with your computer, tablet, and mobile devices

- Print & eBook Best Value Packs

- eBook Deal of the Week – Save up to 50% on featured title

- Newsletter – Be the first to hear about new releases, announcements, special offers, and more

- Register your book – Find companion files, errata, and product updates, plus receive a special coupon* to save on your next purchase

Discounts are applied to the list price of a product. Some products are not eligible to receive additional discounts, so your discount code may not be applied to all items in your cart. Discount codes cannot be applied to products that are already discounted, such as eBook Deal of the Week, eBooks that are part of a book + eBook pack, and products with special discounts applied as part of a promotional offering. Only one coupon can be used per order.

 Pearson